The universe
is <u>yours</u>

Have at it!

Blessings,

WANDING

The very new, very ancient art and science of boldly claiming the life, the love and the prosperity the universe stands ready to provide you.

Our deepest fear is not that we are inadequate.

Our deepest fear is that we are powerful beyond measure.

NELSON MANDELA

For Gary Chandler and Jeff Warburton.

You've shown me that death

is indeed a revolving door.

And for Bobette, my wise companion.

Pages of this edition are printed single-sided

in wanding format for ease of use.

Published by Lostwood Arts Press, Seattle/Salt Lake City

For information, address: Lostwood Arts Press
www.lostwoodarts.com

Printed in the United States Of America

Cover design: Evan Twede

ISBN # 1-56684-666-8

WANDING

The very new, very ancient art and science of boldly claiming the life, the love and the prosperity the universe stands ready to provide you.

EVAN TWEDE

Lostwood

Lostwood Arts Press

SEATTLE / SALT LAKE CITY

CONTENTS

A WORD BEFORE WANDING

It's not unheard of to begin a book by first discussing all the things it won't be about. Such an approach seems prudent here. Wanding is the type of topic certain to carry with it a raft of negative baggage, misconceptions, and superstition – all best put to rest at the outset. And while this book will provide a thorough examination of the practice of wanding, its ancient roots, proper application, and importance for an evolving, spiritual society, we will, nevertheless, begin with everything wanding is not.

Wanding is not sorcery or devil worship. It isn't the exclusive property of any specific theology or denomination. There are no rigid rules, articles of faith, or codes of conduct. Its power isn't reserved for the spiritually elite, the

financially mighty or politically powerful. It doesn't require vows of silence, acts of contrition, sacrifice or even humility. The wood serves all and is a perfect reflection of the divine power of love which makes it function – love which seeks to neither discriminate, nor condemn. It performs as well for the Wicca priestess as it does the Presbyterian minister, marketing representative, saint or sinner. Yet, for all its incomprehensible power, wanding is a very simple, unadorned concept: It is a key, a process for unlocking the spiritual and material treasures of the universe which are now, and always have been, your birthright.

While wanding is not tied to any specific religion or ideology, it is nevertheless a *belief system.* Wanding works. But, it works relative to an individual's belief, or faith in the power which underlies it. In sharing this process, I've witnessed a novice faith quickly mature into a deep, peaceful practition-

er's knowing. It is within this space of quiet confidence and love that the real miracles occur. I welcome you on this path.

Effective practice of this, or any other spiritual art, begins with knowledge. An understanding of what the universe is, how it operates, and why it exists, is essential. You, gentle seeker, may be elated or disappointed to discover a portion of *WANDING* devoted to what may seem overtly theological matters. It's necessary. *WANDING* is part philosophy, part how-to. A little bit Zen, a little bit rock and roll. I advise you to be patient and take things step by step. Without the proper tools, and background, you're just swatting at shadows.

A few other notes. This is not a scholarly text. I approach the subject as a friendly conversation – one in which, admittedly, I do all of the talking, but also one in which I employ personal anecdotes from time to time and the occasional pop-culture reference. I'm confident the informal style won't

detract from the value of the information presented. The power of wanding is unambiguous, objective fact. I see no purpose in approaching it as a mystical cliché, wrapped in pretentious, supernatural language. My interest in bringing this powerful practice public stems from a long-standing desire to see spirituality flourish throughout our global society in a non-denominational, healing form.

I offer a nod of thanks to the Fitchel Society, a group dedicated to the preservation of *Die Ur Methode* (the classic fashion) of wanding, wand use and manufacture.

Finally, in *WANDING*, I refer to the creator in the masculine. Him. He. His. God is, I believe, a balance of attributes which transcends gender as we understand it, and exceeds the limits of our current comprehension. But for reasons of expediency and continuity, I reference the divine in the common, socially familiar form. May she have mercy on me.

1

A SIMPLE ROD OF WOOD

What if you could wave a wand and change the world? What if you knew for a certainty that, by making such an effort, you would create positive change in your life and in the lives of millions of your fellow beings? Would you do it? If you truly believed it were possible, could anything stop you from doing it? The fact that this book has found you answers that question. Wanding is something you have called forth into your space – placing you among a small community of people powerful and open enough to wonder ***what if?***

What lies before you is a road map, a detailed diagram for creating abundance, passion, peace and magic in your life. All of this and more from a simple rod of wood.

Wanding isn't religion. It's the application of knowledge. And, while *wanding* as a term may be new to our current consciousness, it is anything but new to the human experience. As a practice, wanding has been had, lost then recovered by mankind repeatedly over the ages. The wand, itself, has appeared in many forms throughout history and figures in countless doctrines, dogmas and philosophies – spiritual and secular – to this day.

In 1953, Queen Elizabeth received the Royal Scepter, the "ensign of kingly power and justice," at the hands of an archbishop carrying a crosier – a pastoral staff representing his divine authority. Wands have played a pivotal role in spiritual and political governance since before the first Pharaoh assumed the throne. Wands are a worldly symbol of other-worldly power because they are a literal connection to the source from which that power emanates.

Wands, scepters, rods and staffs are featured in the Bible, the Torah, the Koran, the Pali Canon, Babylonian texts, the Bhagavad Gita, Egyptian and Mayan hieroglyphics, Olmec artifacts and countless other sources. References to wands cross the totality of religious writing and thought.

Throughout our shared history, and into the present day, the wise have possessed their wands, the holy, their staffs,

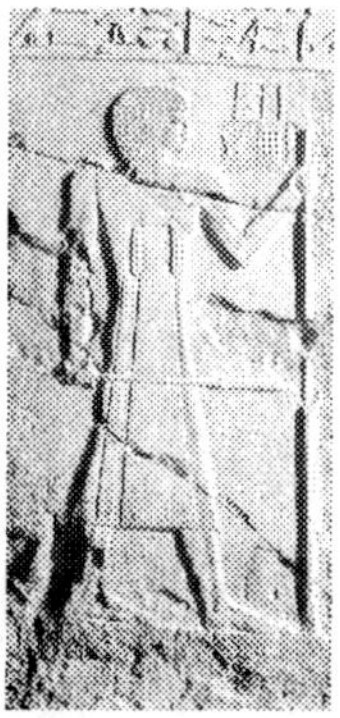

and royal, their scepters – while the rest of the world bowed down in service to them. It begs the question: Why them and not you? If we are all equal in the eyes of God, then why should the common man be excluded from enjoying the same knowledge, or exercising the same spiritual connection? What's wrong with you?

Why shouldn't you have everything you've ever dreamed of – materially and spiritually? Who says you don't deserve to be healthy or wealthy or happy or wise or skinny? In all likelihood, the *who* is you. That *still small voice* reminding you even now that "you're not worthy or righteous enough to deserve universal abundance" is your *own* voice. It isn't God, the devil, or the tyranny of fate keeping you from achieving your desires. The culprit is unquestionably YOU.

The good news is you may now give yourself permission to put aside all issues of unworthiness and limiting beliefs, and simply take possession of the abundance which is now, and has always been, your birthright. You were born worthy of everything the universe holds and nothing you've fouled up since arriving in mortality has done anything to change that. God isn't an accountant keeping score. He doesn't care whether you love Him, hate Him,

or dismiss Him as myth. He accepts you and that's enough.

So consider this your new moment. The past is past. There is only now. This is the time to boldly claim that the life, the love, the answers and the prosperity you seek are now yours to enjoy in whatever proportions you wish, in whatever form you imagine, and in whatever time frame you desire. It's all yours for the cost of a single, focused, affirmative *claim.* This isn't selfishness. This isn't sin. It's simply the way the universe works.

Wands.

To the mortal, a wand is a focal point, a visualization tool, a physically manifest invocation of spirit energy. To those residing in spirit, a wand is a ringing telephone. The act of wanding separates your intentions from the steady stream of routine wants and wishes to the realm

of clear, focused, imperative priority.

In the Tarot, the wand represents fire in the spiritual sense, a link to the realms of light, and the power of truth. In another account, wands symbolize spiritual aspirations, creative energy, hopes, material wealth, and desires. Wands represent ambition, enthusiasm and enterprise with an emphasis on the higher spiritual verities of life as opposed to the mundane and dim light of mortality. Popular culture has had its effect on our perception of wands. In movies and books they appear as ornate talismans encrusted with crystals, metals, leather and all forms of arcane mystical decoration. An authentic wand is a bit less impressive.

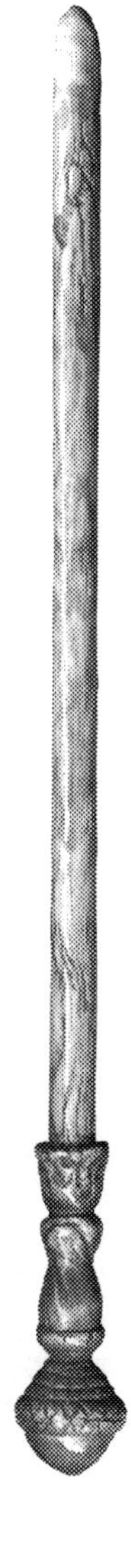

Symbolism in the wand.

An authentic wand starts with simple, unadorned wood – symbolic of the choice we made in spirit to put aside our glory and incarnate into the "rough clay of flesh." A wand has five parts – one for each of the five elements. The bulbous end represents earth. The handle symbolizes water, the shaft, fire and the tip, air. Inverted, it takes on a phallic appearance indicative of fertility and renewal. Anciently, the LANTS, or tip, was regularly scratched bare to allow the free flow of spirit energy in and out of the wand. It's interesting to note that the modern black and white illusionist wand retains vestiges of these early doctrines for wandcrafting. The tips of today's typical magic wands are banded in white – an oblique, though lost reference to the practice of scratching.

These are the parts of an authentic wand:

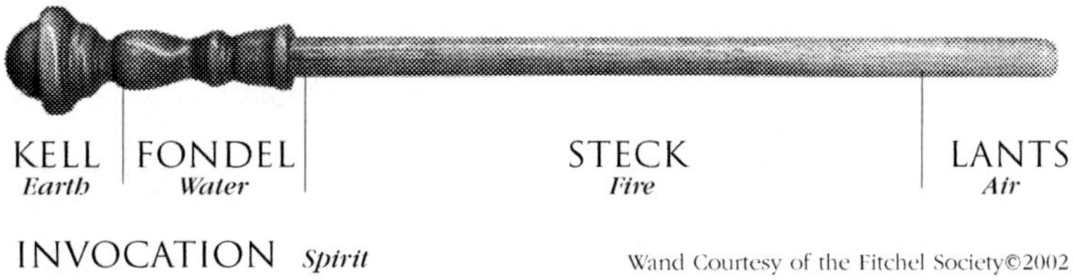

Wand Courtesy of the Fitchel Society©2002

There are many competing concepts of what wands should look like, but there is no right or wrong wand – only what works. In modern Wicca, willow wands are used. Ancient European Druidism favored oak and mistletoe. The Magi used cedar. The type of wood utilized in wanding is less a factor than the skill and clear intent of the individual wielding it. The key is to follow your *knowing*. It will direct you to the wand which has chosen you.

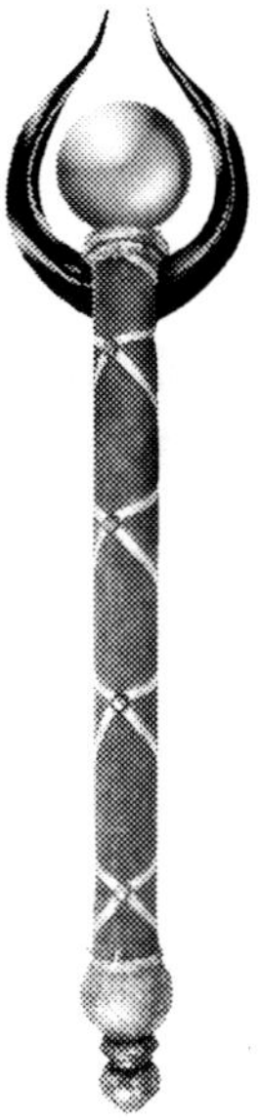

The winding.

The source of the current word *wand* derives from the archaic *weig* – a word which denotes both "wand" and "to wind." It is the root from which the modern Wicca takes its name. Indeed, it is still prescribed practice today to introduce a corporal – or human element during wand creation.

This takes the form of a *winding* of the wandcrafter's hair embedded in the handle where the FONDLE meets the STECK – the principle being that this link to the mortal body, creates a familiar *domicile* where the spirit can dwell while providing service to the wand. With the introduction of spirit as the final step, the five elements of earth, water, fire, air and spirit are complete and the circle closed.

Die Ur Methode, or classic fashion of wand creation, dictates that wands aren't finished until they have been consecrated and *named* by an individual known as a *Listener.* The Listener hears the name by which the wand wishes to be addressed during its period of service. It is this name which the *practitioner* later ceremoniously invokes to invite the spirit into service of the wood. To a practitioner, a wand is a dear friend and is treated as any other loving, reciprocal relationship.

Wanding.

Wanding is the process of harnessing universal power towards creating the results you desire in your life. It's a proven method for focusing your own energy, calling forth divine energy, and communicating more effectively with interested parties in the spirit realms. Because, without the spirit active in the process, a wand is just wood. Wanding distills and directs the potent energy of affirmation, but is far beyond wishful thinking or creative visualization. It's a ceremonial process whereby you lay claim to the spiritual and material treasures of the universe. Wanding is positive affirmation taken to a cosmic level – one in which you literally draw forth the blessings of heaven. In order for you to wand with power, you must first possess the confidence and authority that only knowledge can provide. You should also be properly introduced to the power driving it. At long last.

2

GOD, GUIDES AND THE LAW OF UNIVERSAL SUPPLY

This is a bit presumptuous, but I am going to explain in a few pages that which has been misunderstood by the masses in millions of pages. It's time to meet your maker.

Pull a hair from your head. Look closely at it. That hair is you – you in the *physical* sense. In fact, that hair is as much YOU as any other single part which combines to constitute your body. It's as much YOU as your heart or your foot. Hair is a unique, beautiful combination of cells which have gathered for the sole purpose of being HAIR. Some cells congregate to become a liver while others form bone,

but all are required in order to create a body. Every cell is unique in its mission, and essential to the proper functioning of the whole. The cells which make up your hair are no more or less prestigious than the ones which created your retinas or your pancreas. They are all equally vital aspects, elements, or *individuations* of the body you currently occupy. You don't look at your hair and say, "That's me." But perhaps you should. Within every one of your cells is the grand design, the blue print for making a human *body.* In your body alone resides the information for building billions of bodies. And within each of those billion bodies the information for another billion and so on. When you begin to grasp this concept, an understanding of God is not far off.

We are God. God is us.

We have a tendency to think of ourselves in the micro (small)

and God in the macro (big). After all, he created our universe. He may have created an infinite number of universes. He's certainly larger and grander than we will ever be. Right? Well, no actually. You have more in common with God than you think.

Think of yourself as the cell and the universe the body. As a cell, you are allowed to make certain assumptions about your place in the body and indulge yourself in a number of expectations. Take your own body for example. Your cells aren't concerned with issues of worthiness or guilt. They simply go about the business of being what they are – the building blocks of brains and hearts and fingernails. They *expect* your body to supply their needs. It's symbiotic. The cells make up the body. The body provides for the cells – without prejudice, disapproval or bias for as long as the cells require it. Cells don't have to qualify for nutrition from the body or

be worthy of oxygen, plasma or antibodies. It's all supplied on demand. Your body was created as a supply system for your individual cells. Your cells, in turn, have organized to create the body which now serves you. But you are not your body. *You* are something vastly different.

When you step into your automobile, you don't become the car. You utilize the car. You drive it. It gets you where you want to go. When your car has exhausted its useful life, you replace it with one that works better. You don't mourn your car's loss, or visit it at the wrecking yard on the anniversary of your parting. If you're sane, you move on and, in all likelihood, never give it more than a passing thought. Bodies are like that. They're transitory, biological devices which enable spirit beings to gather mortal experiences. Your spirit *drives* them. In the macro, God is the driver and we are the vehicle. We are the aspects – the

individuations – which combine to create what God is. We enable God to experience Himself. We provide Him movement. He, in turn, sustains our spirits – allowing us to progress and experience *ourselves*. He provides *us* movement.

Religion and philosophy teach us that we're imperfect, natural, mortal beings seeking a spiritual experience. But that's backwards. We're *spirit* beings seeking an imperfect, natural, *mortal* experience. And not just one mortal experience. As many as it takes. You see, you're not here to qualify for eternal life. You're already in the thick of it.

You are eternally progressing.

Reincarnation, or soul evolution, is a difficult concept for many to grasp. To some it means the actual cycle of mortal life, death and rebirth as a continuing, repeatable process. For others, it indicates a series of steps which have been

proceeding since the emergence of our intelligences in the spirit realms – of which a mortal experience plays an essential role. Whichever way you view the eternal journey of spirit, one fact is clear: we chose mortal life. Mortality provides us the challenges and experiences our spirits not only desire – but require. The ability to incarnate into mortal bodies literally saves our souls.

Stand on one foot for sixty seconds. See how that feels. Now hold your breath for thirty seconds. All in all the exercise took less than two minutes. Yet, those brief moments seemed endless while you were caught up in them. Now imagine sitting in a movie theater, watching *The Fellowship Of The Ring* continuously for an entire year. You never get to leave. You eat, drink, shave, shower and sleep there. Eight showings a day – every day for 365 days. Fortunately, you picked a good film. *The Fellowship Of The Ring* is one of the

better tales ever brought to the screen. But even the devoted fan will quickly get his or her fill of it and want to move on. By the end of the year, which included all 2,920 nonstop viewings, even the most ardent *Lord Of The Rings* fanatic would want to rip Tolkien and all of his damned books to shreds – having gone hopelessly insane during showing #112. And that's just one year. Imagine a *Fellowship Of The Ring* non-stop marathon lasting thirty years. Seventy. Try to fathom the toll such a thing would take on the mind, body and spirit. Like other experiences in life, endless repetition and lack of movement quickly turn any heaven into hell. Say you were to take just one step every trillion years. Even at that imperceptibly slow pace, you would still eventually traverse the entire universe in every direction an *infinite* number of times. That's the reality of eternity. Mortal incarnations save our souls from stagnation and spiritual death.

The Universe is there for us to use.

We often think of the universe as the canopy of galaxies over our heads on a clear summer evening. That's the manifest, or physical universe – an endless expanse of rock, hydrogen and frigid cold. This is not what is meant when we say *universe*. For our purposes, think of the universe like the body we spoke of earlier. The universe exists solely to give us things. That's it. It's there for us to use. It provides us with the material and spiritual support, inspiration and opposition required to accomplish our purposes in coming to earth. It's a supply system – a cash machine dispensing limitless currency without prejudice or restrictions. Punch in your PIN and take what you want when you want it. No questions asked. No explanations required. No tests of worthiness. Assistance from the universe is not something you are expected to grovel for. It's yours for the taking. All that is

required of you is a single, positive, imperative claim on whatever you feel is lacking from your life experience in that moment. Abundance is your birthright.

To make the experience real and meaningful, you chose to incarnate into mortality without any memory of your spiritual nature. You arrived on earth without your recollections, but not without your glory, your prestige, or your power. You are a literal aspect of God. You're royalty. If you were a prince or princess, you wouldn't be forced to beg for firewood when you wanted to have your chamber warmed on a chilly evening. You would snap your fingers and expect the assembled staff to see to your comforts immediately.

As an adolescent, I performed on stage in several productions. At no point was I ever required to gather the costumes, props, lights, programs and refreshments. I didn't have to build the stage, sew the curtains or hang the lights.

I simply arrived on time expecting to find all the elements in place. If a scene called for a dog house, it was provided. I didn't have to earn the dog house based on the merits of my performance. I had the right to expect that it would be there when I needed it. In fact, if the curtain was rising and a prop wasn't in place, I had the duty to demand it be found in time for the performance. We don't have to earn universal abundance. We simply claim it. We are, all of us, currently in a performance we call mortal, physical life. But unlike the works of Williams, Coward or Shakespeare, ours is a production of our own design where we call the shots, amend the script and change the characters and scenery at will – moment to moment. The stage was set, dressed and prepared for us before we arrived on earth, but we are free to do with it what we will. We are always at choice. We are the directors. We incarnated on earth to complete ourselves

through new experiences. There is no right or wrong way to gather them. God provided the universe as a support system to enable us to mount as many productions as we wish as often as it suits us.

You are worthy.

As a population, we don't view ourselves as worthy. We don't view God as loving. We don't perceive this life as a growth experience. Instead, we see it as an obedience test, and hate ourselves for our repeated failures. We've become fallen, doomed souls whose only hope for an afterlife resides in the careful adherence to religious principles. Our self-hate has radiated outward, becoming institutionalized, synthesized, widely-broadcast, global hate. It's no wonder so much of the world worships a vengeful, jealous, punitive God. It was created in our own image. Fortunately, you now

have permission to let that image go. If there is a word capable of describing God in our language, the word is love absolute and without condition. Worthiness isn't something you prove. It's something you are.

To God and to our spirits, mortal incarnations are experiences, nothing more. There is no *pass / fail.* Our souls are never in danger of being lost to the pit, purgatory or anything else. To the immortal, mortality is but an exercise.

One afternoon I heard my ten-year old son screaming. He was playing a video game I'd purchased for him as a birthday present and things weren't going well. Time after time, he had failed to surmount a particular obstacle – a deep, jagged pit. His character died before my eyes twenty times. With tear-streaked cheeks, the little boy repeated the same steps until at last, he realized what he had been doing wrong. He got past that peril, and within time, all others that

followed. Today the game is at the bottom of a stack because once my son mastered it, he became bored of it. He has since moved to other, more challenging pursuits. Our spirits are no less inquisitive and hungry for new experiences than a ten-year old child. I should point out that although I offered my son an occasional suggestion, at no point in the game-playing exercise did I banish him to his room for failing to jump that pit. He was never held accountable for the number of mushrooms he disintegrated or flaming rodents he killed with his singing sword. Instead, he was loved, validated and appreciated for his resolve to stick with the problem until it was solved. Our mortal lives are like the game. To die in this world is to arrive back at the couch, so to speak – ready to take it all on again if need be, or move on if we decide there are no more lessons left to be learned here. God doesn't damn us *to* failure or *for* failure. He

bought us the game and is content to watch us play it out. We are creating this mortal experience, our play, moment to moment. We change our reality with the power of our own intent. This is important to realize should you find yourself in a relationship, a job, or any other situation that isn't working for you. The past doesn't exist. You are not bound to it. The only moment there is – and ever will be is NOW. You exist in the present tense. If something isn't working in your life, create a new life from this moment on.

Guides and other spirits.

As is the case in mortality, there are people on the other side, too – interested parties with whom we have shared countless moments. These people are as real and meaningful to us as our siblings, spouses, friends or parents are now. None of us comes to earth without the assistance of such

individuals. They are called guardian angels, spirit helpers or guides. Their function is to inspire us to stay on the path we mapped out for ourselves before coming to earth. Everything serves a purpose in mortality. There are no accidents. I used to bristle when I'd hear someone say that. Certainly there *were* accidents. It's one thing for the baby to die, but why did she have to be slowly crushed by a cement truck? Today I realize that everything which happens in our lives has value. If one of my purposes in coming to earth was to learn forgiveness, then I will encounter people who will wrong me. These people aren't just there arbitrarily. They are there because they agreed to be there. And out of love for me, they are willing to put in an appearance as a thorn in my side. When you come to view negative individuals in your life as partners in your growth – spirits who love you enough to stretch you – then you are less inclined to

take life's insults as personally. You are suddenly free to love your enemies and pray for those who spitefully use you. You are relieved of the terrible burden of having to formulate judgments about the habits, lifestyles and choices of people around you. All of which begs the question; "If everyone is performing their perfect function, is there such a thing as actual *evil?"*

Does evil exist in the universe, or are the people currently raping the land and each other merely fulfilling a promise to make life miserable for everybody else? It's the quintessential mystery of life. If evil is necessary for our progress, is it really *evil* in the traditional sense? Consider the video game example. Were a company to create a game where everything progressed smoothly and serenely from the beginning to the end with no bumps, no ripples and no surprises, would anyone bother playing it? Where would

drama be without an antagonist? *Hamlet* would be a Danish documentary. Overcoming obstacles is the purpose of the exercise. The evil that men do serves us. It inspires greatness, courage and sacrifice in those sworn to defeat it. It forges strength through suffering and can lead to the highest graces which are forgiveness and compassion. Opposition in the physical world is the barbell which exercises the muscle of our spirit. It's what makes the mortal journey worth taking. The balance between good and bad is perfect in mortality. But what about when the spirit completes the mortal exercise? Does evil rise with it? Is there evil in spirit?

Negativity exists on the other side in the form of base, or unevolved energies. The darkness which resides in the spiritual realms, however, is tied to the mortal plane. Because spirits have individual agency, they are free to

remain bound to the earth after their lives here are completed. Such energies do linger among us after death, enslaved by addiction, or guilt, or the lusts which ruled them in mortality. These confused spirits could enter the light and take their place with the angels at any time. But their fear of a God's judgment or a devil's Hell prevents them from seeing the brilliant light of perfect love. And so they tarry. They may be in denial regarding their status. They may be confused from the sudden trauma of their deaths, or retain unfulfilled desires their abrupt passings denied them. There may simply be too much anger and hostility present in these souls for them to feel comfortable about moving into a space of peace and divine love. It is souls in this category which account for much of the haunting, poltergeist activity and demonic possession phenomena. These are the spirits often moving your ouija boards and making your parlor games

exciting. They are energies to avoid unless their negativity in your life serves your purposes. It's important to realize that though these darkness dwellers possess the ability to vex the living during their mortal sojourns, they are powerless to impede the progress of a spirit unless that individual chooses it as a lesson.

Because everyone is at choice, some souls progress along their paths at different rates than others. Spirits may choose to return to earth to re-experience mortality, or opt to move forward. Many serve as guides – spirit energies who agreed to assist us in achieving our goals while on earth. Guides are the source of divine magick. They serve up the experiences, and spiritual and material support we require as participants in the grand game of mortality. They won't insulate you from challenges which facilitate your growth because the negative is as rewarding as the positive. We signed on for

both. You will have difficult experiences in your life until the moment comes that you overcome your need for them. Your guides inspire your spirit into making those life choices which promote your progress. It's important to establish a loving, appreciative dialog with your guides as early in life as possible.

One last comment about guides. These energies are your friends. They are equal to you in the eternal perspective. They are people whom you love and who love you. They don't judge you for being human anymore than you judge an infant for soiling a diaper. The verities of life are well understood in spirit realms. Therefore, if I can add one personal word of counsel, it is this. Take the time to thank them for the good and the bad things in your life. Speak it out loud as if they're in the room. Everything that happens to you enlarges you in a way you may not appreciate until your

eyes are re-opened. Remember to thank the creator as well. Bear in mind that He neither requires nor desires your protestations of inadequacy and self-loathing. He understands mortal life. He appreciates the importance of the lessons of mortality. Thank Him as you would a cherished friend. The good news is that He is all that and more. He's only about love and acceptance and is not someone you ever need to fear. So, to review, here are the essentials you need to realize about the universe in order for your own practice of wanding to have power:

1. *God is us. We are one.*
2. *The universe is a supply system intended for your use. Abundance is your birthright. There is enough for all.*
3. *We are worthy. There is nothing to prove.*
4. *We live in the eternal moment of NOW and create our reality moment to moment.*
5. *We are spirit beings having a mortal experience.*
6. *We are assisted by interested parties in spirit.*

3 PREPARATION FOR WANDING

If you listen with your spirit, you'll notice that some places carry a unique spiritual resonance, a separateness, a heightened vibration caused by the synchronicity of the spirits of the people within – past and present. Think of how you feel when you enter a cathedral, or mosque, a synagogue, or sweat lodge. There is a reverence in these places. A separateness. This type of spiritual separation is not an essential component in wanding, but is very helpful toward focusing your energies. I advise you to establish a special place you can escape to – a door you can close on the heavy vibrations of the outside world. Call it your sanctuary or your retreat. I call it a wanding space.

Creating your wanding space.

You'll know it when you feel it. There is probably a location you are visualizing right now which carries the very qualities I've been describing. If not, a special space can be created.

Here are a few things to look for. Seek out a warm, secure, private location that is easily accessible to you when the impulse to wand strikes. Public properties are not recommended. Wanding outdoors is an exhilarating, powerful experience, but for your own personal wanding space, a familiar, consistent, comfortable place is best. The first thing to do upon selecting your space is to smudge the area. This spiritual cleansing involves burning a wand of sage and allowing the smoke to permeate every corner. Visualize the smoke as pure radiant light. It is often helpful in visualizations to add the component of sound. As you're imagining

the space filled with shimmering light, include the sound of lightly tinkling bells. When you've completed the smudge, it's time to claim the space. This is accomplished through a simple prayer, or invocation of your higher power, and can take any form you deem appropriate. I include a standard ceremony below, but feel at peace and choice to improvise. Remember, wanding works on the principle that you are creating your reality moment to moment. If what you're doing establishes the proper resonance with your spirit, then it's right for you. Ceremony and ritual are important aspects of any effective spiritual practice, so don't feel embarrassed or awkward as you begin to apply them. Always observe any spiritual process with sincerity, faith and a sense of gratitude. Avoid including people in your spiritual practices who are not at your level. It's not that these are rites which require secrecy, but the skeptical tend to carry with them a

very heavy, spirit-dampening energy. Enroll them into your personal vision as your spirit dictates, but don't expect them to swallow a chunk of meat when milk is the most they can manage. Divine love is all inclusive. Include everyone in your life and circle of love, but be selective whom you invite into your sacred space.

A CLEANSING CEREMONY

Through the power of divine love, I claim and cleanse this space for the purposes of light and truth. I welcome all spirits of eternal love and demand all agents and energies which seek darkness to depart. I call forth protection into this space. Only light, love and learning exist here. I boldly claim, declare, and decree that this space is worthy, sound and receptive to the workings of light — Now.

The power of Now.

Now? What's this *Now* business? The idea of making such demands on the divine seems ludicrous and sacrilegious when considered from the viewpoint of scarcity – that doctrine which states we are so indebted to God as to never be worthy of His approval or His blessings. But that isn't how God or the universe operates. When you finally succeed in distancing yourself from the limiting delusions of unworthiness, you discover a being at the center of creation quite different from the one you were taught to fear – a being of warmth, humor, understanding and optimism. God created the process of universal, infinite supply as an extension of His own perfected acceptance and love. Gaining the spiritual and material treasures of the universe is as simple as clear, focused, positive intent. The universe awaits your requests, but requires you to state them in unambiguous, imperative terms.

Choose your words carefully. Don't think of the universe, *the universal supply system*, as a conscious person capable of reading between the lines. The universe is more like a mechanical device which hears only what you tell it. That can be a blessing and a curse depending how the request is framed. To the universe and everything contained within, there is only NOW. Yesterday doesn't exist. Two seconds ago doesn't exist. Our memories trick us into thinking there is something besides the present moment, but that isn't reality. Think back to when you first learned to ride your bicycle. As it was occurring, there was no past or future to it. It was simply the moment you were in. It was just as much NOW to you back then as is the moment you read the word NOW on this page. You think there is a past, because your memory stores your moments for review and processing. But existence is really a series of events which all occur

in the same, single, eternal moment of NOW. There is no other moment. This is important to realize as you put forth your desires to the universe. Concentrate on placing everything you say in the proper context and speak the language the universe understands – which is the *present tense.* For this reason, avoid the word *will.*

"My mother will stop being deathly ill and will recover completely."

There are many problems associated with that request. This is what the universe heard: ***"Will be deathly ill. Will recover completely."*** The word *will* implies a nebulous future outcome – a moment which doesn't exist in the vocabulary of the universe. *Will* denotes a continuation throughout the eternal moment of Now. Instead of putting an end to your mother's illness, the universe perpetuates it. The universe isn't unsympathetic. It just does what you say. To the letter.

Speaking the language of Now.

This is the proper way to achieve the result of ending your mother's illness according to the language of Now:

"Divine love is doing its perfect work. My mother is healthy now." Do you see the difference? Nowhere in that sentence is there any reference to future outcomes. I didn't speak of the disease. I simply stated the desired result as though it had already happened. Always avoid vocalizing the negative and steer clear of words such as *can't, won't, don't,* and *not.* Approach all of your declarations only from the positive.

Dressing your space.

Your wanding space should reflect your personal tastes and attitudes. If you worship Jesus Christ through the Blessed Virgin, include their images. If you are into an earth religion, or Buddhism, or Shamanism, decorate your space with those

icons, totems, talismans and amulets which have power for you. If you are a bottom-line type not given to ceremony or superstition, surround yourself with images of the results you wish to achieve. Put the picture of the Porsche on your wall. There is no right or wrong way to set up your wanding space. There is only what works best for you.

Involve your senses. Burn incense, use aromatic oils, candles or anything else which will serve to separate you from the mundane, everyday world beyond the door of your sacred space. Music can be very effective in creating the proper resonance for communication with spirit. I advise against music with a definite rhythm or structure. Avoid music which is familiar to you, because you will find yourself transported back to the memories associated with it. You can find an excellent selection of appropriate music in new age bookstores which is specifically created to facilitate

meditation and spirit travel. Keep the lights low and soothing. If you are burning anything in an enclosed area, be mindful of proper ventilation and fire safety. If you prefer to stand, then stand. If kneeling, reclining or assuming an erect yogic posture works best, by all means, do what works.

Prepare your spirit.

This is the moment to throw off the heavy vibrations of mortal concerns. If you are a person who prays, do so. Invoke the spirit of God into your presence. If you chant, repeat your mantra. If you pray the rosary or ceremonial beads as a regular practice in your life, don't hesitate to do it here. I recommend you include meditation in your spirit preparation. Meditation can synchronize your vibrations with those of the spirit realms. We, as mortal beings, vibrate at a very slow frequency. Spirit operates at a far higher, faster level.

Your guides will lower their vibrations for you, but your communication with them will be enhanced and your wanding more fruitful when you are able to meet them halfway.

As humans, we always have many files open and tapes running in our minds. Meditation allows us to effectively block out the noise and clarify our thought energy. Here is a sample meditation which is very effective in raising your spiritual vibrations for effective communion with your guides.

Before you begin, make certain you're comfortable – but not so comfortable that you're likely to fall asleep. Apprentice meditators usually succumb quickly, but over time, the process becomes second-nature. Set apart at least thirty minutes per session and plan on making it a weekly habit at least. Wear loose-fitting clothing which keeps you at a comfortable body temperature. Remove your jewelry, take

off your shoes, belts and bulky items you may have in your pockets.

You may wish to dictate the following process into a tape recorder if you aren't experienced at meditation. Play it back at a low level. Eventually you will find you can replace the sound of your voice on the tape with the voice in your mind. Be patient. It takes everyone a while to create the desired state through meditation.

A SAMPLE MEDITATION

Seek out your sacred space, or find a place that's quiet and out of the normal stream of disruptions. It may be difficult in a home filled with ringing phones, stereos, pets and family members, but enlist their cooperation. The world can spare you for half an hour. If peace and quiet is simply not to be found within your four walls, purchase a set of head

phones, the type which completely cover your ears. Play soothing music at a low level as you begin to meditate.

I've already discussed the use of candles, incense, aromatic oils, as well as the need for your body to be comfortable and free of any biological needs. Take care of these before beginning. Avoid any mind-altering substances such as drugs, alcohol, or cigarettes.

Take a few deep breaths. Breathe in deeply through your nose and exhale through your mouth. While doing so, imagine that the air coming in is bright, shimmering light. Think of the exhalation as a dark smoke. Breathe spirit and light in – worries, concerns, physical pain and fear out. Let your mind go blank. If thoughts of deadlines, chores or other intruders invade your consciousness, imagine packaging them in a bubble and setting them adrift. Close your eyes. Remember to breathe in through your nose, allowing the air

to go as deeply as possible. Relax your lower abdomen and chest. Let the air fill your entire body. Now, Inhale through your nose for a count of six. Hold it for six. Release the breath through your mouth for six. Do this five times. Inhale the shimmering light, exhale the dank and polluted smoke of physical concern and worry. The light coming into you is purifying your body. As the impurities are exhaled, your cells react with a tingling sensation. Visualize your body slowly becoming the light. Your flesh begins to glow with a soft, warm luminescence. Continue breathing. Now envision a bright, intense light forming at the crown of your head. Feel the heat of it. Smell the particles it charges in the air around you. See how the crown of light illuminates everything in your space. The ceiling, the walls. As you move, the shadows around you move. You are the light.

Now imagine this light moving downward from the

crown of your head into your cranium. See your brain flashing into radiance. Your eyes. If you were to open your eyes, the light would spill forth like the focused beam of a lighthouse. Feel the light moving into your sinuses, your mouth and your throat. Your head is now fully engulfed in this peaceful, radiant, comfortable light. Relax the muscles in your face. Let your eyelids go limp. Allow your lips to part. You feel relaxed and calm.

The light now glides like a thick, radiant syrup down your throat and into your chest. It gathers in your heart. Notice the red glow in your chest becoming orange, then yellow, then white. The center of your chest is now as bright as your head. The light pulses through your arms, as though pumped there by the relaxed rhythm of your heart. Your shoulders begin to glow brightly, your upper arms, your forearms, wrists and hands. The light blazes forth from your

fingertips like searchlights. Roll your fingers gently. See the light casting away the shadows around you. Your upper body is now blazing with the heat and serenity of this healing, calming light. Now visualize this light racing from your neck, down your spine. Light surges throughout your nervous system, reaching into every cell. A pulse of cleansing radiance moves into your lower abdomen. Feel it in your genitals, your upper thighs, knees, lower legs, ankles and feet. Imagine this brilliant, divine light projecting outward from your toes, your fingers, your chest, your eyes and the crown of your head. You are a being of light, as formless as a sunbeam, as light as a thought. Your body has lost all density.

Now, imagine the light that you have become, gathering in radiance. Your form is expanding, enlarging into a sphere of perfected, approved, accepted spiritual light. Now count backward in your mind. 10, 9, 8...you are getting lighter. 7,

6, 5...the gravity of earth can no longer contain you. 4, 3, 2, 1. You are lifting up, soft as a whisper and light as a thought. Your sphere of light passes through the ceiling into a beautiful rainbow. You hear the gentle sound of tinkling bells.

You feel your spirit rising. You are surrounded, awash in beautiful, crimson light. You detect the scent of roses. Remain in this place for a moment. Feel the rose light working itself through you. You feel safe and tranquil. There is peace and love in this light. Now, feel yourself rising once again. The red is giving way to orange. This light feels different. Crisper. There is the subtle aroma of freshly cut orange here. Breathe in the delicate citrus scent. Remain in this orange light for a moment, then allow yourself to rise once again. The orange gives way to yellow. This light fills you with cheer and optimism. Your soul is happy and content. You detect a hint of lemon. Float for a moment in the

lemon light. Let the gentle breeze take you where it will. You are rising once more. The yellow gives way to vivid green. The sweet smell of summer grass surrounds you here, filling you with the carefree feeling of youth. Play in this field of living light. Propel yourself forward and back on the breath of thought. Roll high into the serene, verdant green. Rise again. See how the green slowly becomes teal, then aqua. You are now embraced in a refreshing, blue light. It is pure water and clean air.

Remain in this peaceful place for a moment and drink it in. It cleanses and perfects you. Your light begins to glow even brighter as you rise into gathering indigo.

All fears, cares and concerns are spirited away on a river of indigo. You feel powerful and in control. Your light expands in size, filling the indigo space. You detect an appealing aroma of grape. Your spirit soars in this delicious,

empowering place.

You rise again into clear purple. Grape gives way to lilac. This is the light of truth and justification. You are saturated with a sense of your own divinity. You are worthy. You are prepared to renew your association with the inhabitants of the realm of light. From deep within you, a new light, brighter and more spiritually charged begins to radiate outward. It overcomes the lesser light, then it contracts. You are now a mere point of light. So tiny as to have no diameter, yet so bright that you fill the universe with your brilliance. You now appear among lights that are equally bright. Embrace them. These are your guides. Greet them in spirit. Thank them for their assistance in bringing power to your wand. Listen to what they say to you. Remain with them for a while and commune with them. Don't try to understand their messages, just absorb them. What they tell you will

never be forgotten by your spirit. Bless them for their kindness. Now, they gather around you like swirling embers. Their spirits embrace and validate you. This is a moment of perfect peace, tranquility and acceptance. Slowly the white takes on a lavender hue. You feel yourself drifting downward into purple. You notice the cool feeling of tingling, clear water which appears at the crown of your head. As you descend into indigo, the water rushes over your face. Drifting downward into the beautiful blue, the water splashes against your throat. Into green, you feel the water rushing through your heart. It cleanses the stress and anxiety, flushing it away. You descend lightly, softly down through yellow. The water washes your chest and arms all the way to your fingertips. Orange. Your lower body drinks in the refreshing water as strength and mass begin to gather within you. Now all you see is red. Your body has form, weight

and dimension again. The cool water bathes you, baptizes you in the perfect love of divine spirit. Now count from 1 to 10. 1,2,3,4,5,6,7,8,9,10. Your eyes open on your familiar surroundings, but they no longer seem as they were. The colors are brighter and more vivid. The smells are richer. Your thoughts are clearer. And every object in your space now communicates to you through spirit.

Take a moment to reflect on any messages or inspiration which enter your mind. Make note of them. If you feel you are being directed to a certain course of action, act on this intuition. Many people pray for guidance. It is the precious few who wait around long enough to hear the answer.

4

FINDING YOUR WAND

There are as many types of wands as there are practitioners. The question to ask yourself as you seek out your wand is this: "What has power for me?" If you feel a strong orientation toward natural simplicity, a fallen branch might do nicely. If you're the practical, all-business type, perhaps your expensive Mont Blanc pen will serve. If you're crafty, something hand-carved may create maximum value for you. Technically oriented? Find yourself in steel, wire and glass. There is no right or wrong way to create your wand. There is only what works for you. When it comes to finding a wand, my advice is to clear your mind and listen. Experience has shown me that we don't choose our wands. They choose us.

Hear the call.

For me, *Die Ur Methode*, or classic fashion of wand creation, has power. Its non-denominational, ancient forms appeal to my spiritual sensitivities and satisfy my desire for authenticity. And while I do honor the minds and muscle which have brought our world to its current state of technological achievement, I nevertheless feel the ancients more ably navigated the subtle waters of spirit than we're capable of duplicating today. The mechanized drone of modern society has neutered and numbed those fragile spiritual senses our ancestors took for granted. In many ways, we've lost more than we've gained. It's time to take our power back.

If waving a ball-point pen doesn't appeal to you, here's a somewhat richer, more traditional method for crafting your wand. I've said that wanding is a *belief system.* If what I describe in the following pages isn't something you can

comfortably integrate into your personal spiritual vision, then, as always, follow your spirit.

A simple wand.

The Fitchel (pronounced *Feeshelle*) method calls for three sections of wood taken from different trees. These individual segments signify the domains of mind, body and spirit, and may symbolize other classic trinities as well: the Father, The Son and the Holy Spirit; the sun, moon and stars; Osiris, Isis and Horus; the Green Man, the Goddess and the nurturing earth. The trinity is a recurring theme in nearly every spiritual ideology. The wand itself is carved to symbolize earth, water, fire and air – with the introduction of spirit constituting the fifth element. The process involved in creating a wand, according to *Die Ur Methode,* requires a month to complete – symbolically passing the wood through the

five forms or elements. Wands are begun under the full moon and completed a month later under the full moon. They are consecrated, named, smudged with sage and sealed up against daylight – in preparation for the practitioner's personal invocation ceremony which typically takes place at sun down.

I made the point that the power of wanding is unambiguous, objective fact which functions without the need of supernatural pretension or mystical cliché. I hold to that. Still, I also believe there is power in ceremony and energy in ritual. Observance of sacred processes – whatever they look like to you – heightens our own sense of the spiritual and adds value. Here, then, is one method for crafting a simple wooden wand loosely based on the Fitchel doctrine. If you prefer the genuine article, you're welcome to visit their website at: www.fitchel.com. If your tastes run in a different direction, there are many sites on the internet to turn to.

CREATE YOUR WAND

1. Buy three dowels: Two 3/4" in diameter and one 1/2" in diameter.
2. Cut 1/2" off first large dowel, 3" off the next large dowel and 12" off the smaller dowel.
3. Drill hole 1/2" deep in large dowel end with 1/2" drill bit. Attach short end piece – opposite the hole – with a water-based glue.
4. Pluck a hair. Coil it around the end of the small dowel with a spot of glue.
5. Glue the shaft into the handle.
6. Allow to dry undisturbed overnight.
7. Sand the handle and tip smooth. Create subtle designs and contours if you wish.
8. Apply a water-based paint then re-sand.
9. Rub with clear wax or polish. Buff.
10. Sand or scratch the tip.

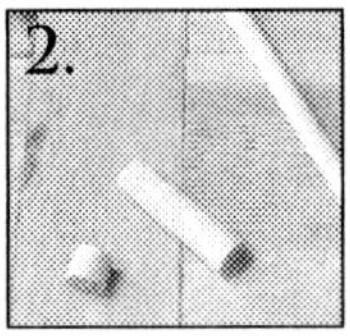

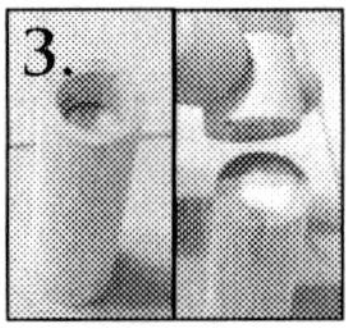

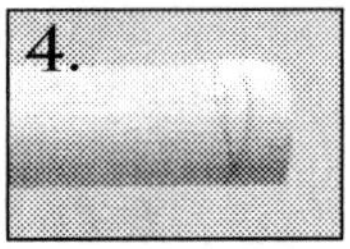

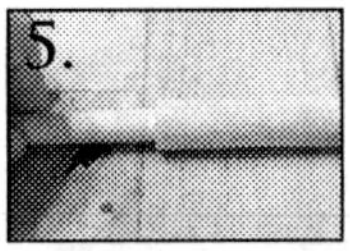

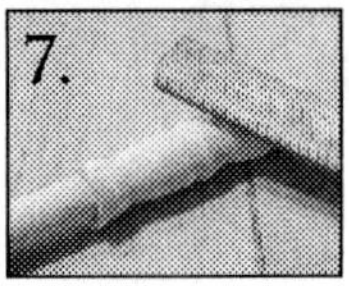

5

THE INVOCATION

This is an optional, but rewarding ceremony which has its roots in antiquity. I recommend you invoke the spirit into your wand in this personal, yet formal exercise. The act of invocation is a deliberate, spirit to spirit re-connection which will have meaning to you as well as to the spirit providing service to your wand. In olden times this service was referred to as *die willkomenheissen.* The welcoming.

The invocation ceremony, or welcoming, is a reunion with the spirit of the wood. Tradition dictates this brief service take place in the outdoors, and under the light of the moon and/or candles. The aim is to create a new and meaningful experience which is separate from your normal day-

light routine. And bear in mind, the ceremony doesn't just create value for you alone. The welcoming is the fulfillment of an agreement you made with the spirit of the wood long ago – a pact initiated before you incarnated on earth. Your relationship will continue throughout mortality and transcend your physical passing. The spirit of your wand is someone dear to you – a soul who has agreed to accompany you and assist you in the good works you will perform in mortality. It has been a long journey for both of you.

The naming.

Your wand has a name. Meditate on what it is. The sound of the vowels and consonants by which the wood wishes to be addressed will come to your mind in meditation. You will know it when you hear it. Guides rarely present names like Ed or Jessica. More common are names that are distinctly

different and separate from the norm. Here is a sampling of names received in spirit. When a name like one of these enters your mind, secure it. Write it down. Then meditate on it. Ask your guides whether it is the name for your wand. You will experience a burning of spirit if the name is correct. If the naming process proves to be too significant an obstacle for you, don't fret. You may email the *Listener* at ***listener@fitchel.com***. The name for the wood will be sought through spirit in your behalf at no charge to you. If you see a name below which calls to you, ask your guides if it would be appropriate to address your wand with it.

Wand names.

Agenoie (A-jen-oy)

Eumarion (Oh-mah-rio)

Larotte (Lah-row)

Cabriotte (Cah-bree-oh)

Dargou (Dar-gow)

Gadrillette (Gah-drel-ay)

Pennshoi (Pun-joy)
Nollencotte (No-len-coh)
Sabonne (Sah-bon)
Tanashette (Tah-na-shay)
Amelon (A-mel-ahn)
Zeniphae (Zen-ee-fay)
Segeauoux (See-jay-oh)
Mollancha (Mole-an-cah)
Varion (Va-ree-own)
Phragenoitte (Fray-jen-oy)
Marialle (Mah-ree-ahl)
Sallerenoux (Sal-ar-en-oh)
Avellonnen (A-vel-oh-nun)
Redeulorre (Re-do-lore)
Erdische (Air-dish-ah)
Demeroux (Deh-mair-oh)
Harreuan (Ha-roon)
Regenne (Re-jen)
Gabriolle (Gah-bree-ole)
Prebrianne (Pre-bree-aan)
Westrialle (Wes-tree-ahl)
Klantalcoux (Clan-tal-coo)
Dorielle (Door-ee-el)
Ellujenta (El-oo-jen-ta)
Kellandroux (Kel-an-droh)
Galtrellen (Gal-trel-ahn)
Sylvanfus (Sil-van-foos)
Moreconai (Mor-eh-con-eye)
Owlentille (Oh-len-til)
Lanoncroix (La-nun-croy)
Netrollesh (Ne-troll-esh)
Gladarelle (Glad-ar-el)

The invocation or "welcoming."

Ceremony and ritual can seem out of place in this age of technical enlightenment. But the value of calling forth spirit energies and stating your clear intention to the universe is as relevant and vital as ever. Ceremony serves and empowers you. It places you in the proper spiritual space. The following invocation hails from ancient forms, but its power is derived from the spirit of divine love which only exists in the moment of NOW.

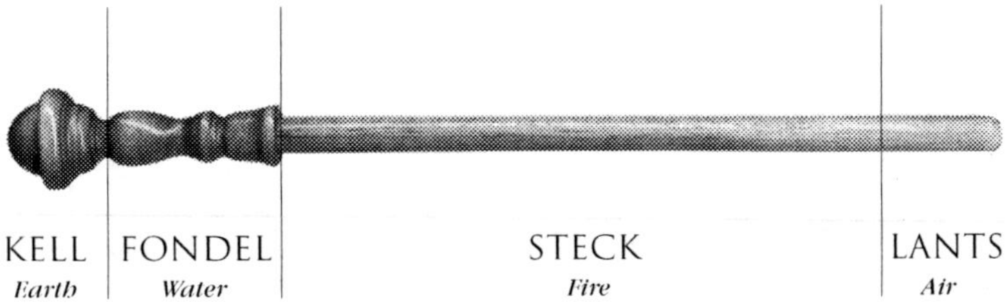

The welcoming is a time of celebration. You may invite like-minded loved-ones and fellow wanding practitioners to take part. Again, this is most powerfully experienced in the out-

doors under a canopy of moonlight. But where that's not possible, try to create a newness to your surroundings. I advise against performing the welcoming in the harsh light of the sun. You will need to prepare some soil, a candle and matches, and a glass of pure water. If this process doesn't appeal to you, improvise your own welcoming ceremony based on what intuition directs. There is no right or wrong.

Holding your wand aloft in your right hand, present it to the moon and stars.

Speak aloud:

I raise thee to the heavens and invoke the spirit
of all light and creation to guide me.

FACE NORTH:

Take the dirt of the earth and sprinkle it on the Kell.

Speak aloud.

I consecrate thee of the earth and invoke the spirit of the
nurturing ground. I call thee forth into the wood.

W A N D I N G

FACE WEST:

Take up the pure water and pour it over the Fondel.

Speak aloud:

I consecrate thee of the water and invoke the spirit of the draught (draft) of life. I call thee forth into the wood.

FACE SOUTH:

Take up a candle and pass the Steck through the flame three times. Speak aloud:

I consecrate thee of the fire and invoke the spirit of the radiant flame. I call thee forth into the wood.

FACE EAST:

Release a breath of air upon the Lants.

Speak aloud:

I consecrate thee of the air and invoke the spirit of the four winds. I call thee forth into the wood.

Hold the wand high into the East.

Bringing the wand from sky to earth, repeat the name of the wand thrice.

(If the name were *Sarlotte*, you would then say:)

I call thee forth from the glory of the All into the womb of this consecrated wood.

I welcome and embrace thee. I welcome and entreat thee. I welcome and invite thee.

Sarlotte into the world.
Sarlotte into the wood.
Sarlotte into the wand.

We are now one in earth, air, fire, water and spirit.

Make the shape of a five-pointed star representing the five elements.

Speak aloud:

Upon the five elements, I boldly claim, declare and decree: Divine love is doing its perfect work.
The spirit Sarlotte is in the wand.
I thank thee for wandering a piece with me.

That completes the welcoming. When initiating a wanding session in the future, you will call forth the spirit of the wood with these words from the ceremony: (If the name were *Arbonne*, you would speak aloud:)

Arbonne into the world.
Arbonne into the wood.
Arbonne into the wand.

Once a wand has been consecrated and the spirit called forth, it is appropriate to wand at any time of the day or night. Wanding rituals don't have to look a certain way, and may take whatever form best serves the practice of your art. There are certain wanding basics you should familiarize yourself with before you begin.

6

WANDING TECHNIQUES

Wanding can be used to achieve many goals – physical, emotional, or spiritual. It can effectively produce material changes in your life, create satisfying relationships, induce feelings of calm, clarity and confidence into difficult situations, and heal you and those around you – body, mind and spirit.

We have a tendency to downplay the mind, as though it were a second-class citizen with no real impact on who we really are or what we're all about. But while in your mortal body, the mind carries a lot of weight. It can inspire you to soar, or keep you locked down – stuck and unable to move.

The mind plays tricks on you and on itself. This is because it relies on the brain to gather information through the senses. But the brain doesn't discriminate. The brain is a biological machine.

While in a dream state, events can seem so real to the mind that they trigger the brain to make the body react to them. In dreams, your body is caught up in the drama, believing what it sees and feels as though it were actually experiencing it. Pulse rates rise. Your body sweats. You cry out, or jerk violently as though falling. As far as your mind and body are concerned, you really ARE being chased by a tiger or plunging off a cliff.

Think of hot apple pie with vanilla ice cream. Just the mention of delicious, fresh-baked pie unleashes a flood of sensory images. Instantly, you get the complete visual picture. You imagine how it tastes, the sweet, spicy aroma

which fills the kitchen. You experience how it feels in your mouth – the blending of textures and temperatures. You hear the sound of the fork clinking against the plate as it breaks the crust. You envision the ice cream melting into milk where it and the pie intersect. Right now your salivary glands are responding to this input as though it were reality. Your stomach is growling at the thought of it.

What happened? Your mind tricked your body. And now your body will run with it. Pie is now on your mind. In all likelihood, you will find a way to have a slice of hot apple pie within hours. What you have just done is taken a thought and made it a reality. This is something intriguing about how our bodies work. They naturally, automatically respond to sensory input – sights, sounds, feel, and taste – as well as emotions like fear, love, hate and envy. All of these trigger specific chemical responses in the brain that

the body runs with. The end result is that your mind and body combine to create your reality. The same principle is true in wanding. The only difference is, instead of drawing upon the power of the mind to affect the body, you draw upon the power of the spirit to affect the universe.

It's a threadworn cliché that whatever the mind can believe, it can achieve. But it's undeniably true on the physical level. Wanding takes this same power of positive visualization and boosts it to the cosmic level. Because, when I said "in wanding you draw upon the power of spirit to affect the universe," I meant it literally.

Drawing forth a new reality.

Wanding is a key to the law of universal supply. It is a tool which enables you to access the power of creation by *drawing* it forth from the source.

W A N D I N G

Now that you have blessed and prepared your space, invoked the spirit into the wood, and brought your own spirit into harmony through meditation, you're ready to take your first step toward creating a new reality. Again, I feel I need to remind you that there is no right or wrong way to wand. I will assert, however, that what I'm about to describe *works*. Here is one wanding process:

How to wand:

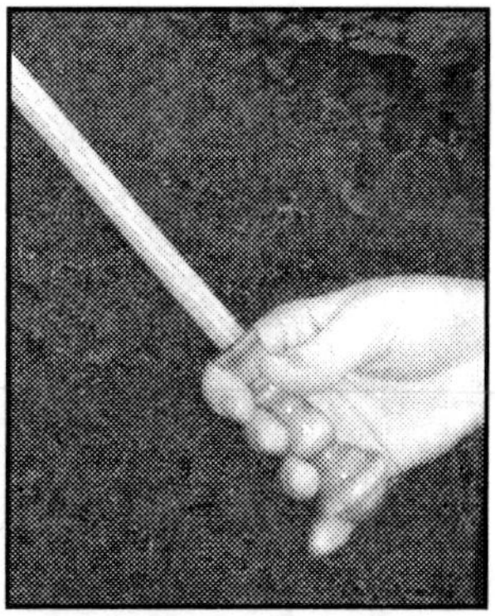

Take the wand in your hand, holding it gently by the Fondel with the pads of your fingers and thumb. Don't grasp it like a racquet or hammer. Be mindful of the power working within the wood. Show it respect and care as you handle your wand. Fill your heart with acceptance and love.

1. CALL FORTH THE SPIRIT INTO THE WOOD

This is accomplished by repeating the phrase from the invocation ceremony. It becomes the standard entreaty to spirit at the beginning of a wanding session. If the name were *Dargau*, you would say:

"Dargau in the world.
Dargau in the wood.
Dargau in the wand."

2. INVOKE YOUR HIGHER POWER.

This can be whatever works best for you. It should be a simple acknowledgment of your God, or higher power. If the result you wish to create is more passion and power in your relationship, this is how you would begin: *"Divine love is doing its perfect work in my relationship with (name.)"*

3. DRAW THE OBJECT OF YOUR DESIRE.

As you are vocalizing your claim, employ your wand as you would a painter's brush on canvas. What this does is produce a physically manifest symbol for the universe which represents your desired outcome. The drawing needn't be complicated. Be certain to repeat the pattern with your wand a minimum of five times while making your vocal declaration. Since the issue we're examining is of a rela-

tionship nature, a shape as simple as a heart would suffice. Feel free to express yourself in any manner you see fit. Make your drawing as complex and detailed as you like if that serves you. If you are interested in creating a material possession, it is appropriate to introduce a photograph of that object, then trace its outline while you make your declaration.

4. SET FORTH YOUR CLAIM.

You don't cast "spells" in wanding. You assert your rightful *claim.* You are in the driver's seat. You create your reality moment to moment. Abundance is your birthright. This is not the moment to be meek. Set forth your clear intention with power and authority: *"I boldly claim, declare, and decree..."*

5. STATE YOUR DESIRES CLEARLY. BE SPECIFIC.

Remember, there is no *will* in the universal vocabulary. We are all in the eternal moment of NOW and you must state your desires in positive, present-tense terms. Avoid negativity.

"...that we experience an abundance of joy, excitement, unity, honesty, adventure, friendship, passion, trust and love..."

6. SEAL YOUR CLAIM.

Specify your time frame in no uncertain terms: *"...Now!"*

7. EXPRESS YOUR GRATITUDE.

Abundance may be your birthright, but gratitude is the key. Treat your relationship with the spirit in your wand in the same way you treat any loving relationship. The traditional benediction at the end of a wanding session goes out to God, the universe and your guide working through the wood:

"I thank thee for walking a piece with me."

So, viewed together, the claim becomes:

"Divine love is doing its perfect work in my relationship with (name.) I boldly claim, declare, and decree that we experience an abundance of joy, excitement, unity, honesty, adventure, friendship, passion, trust and love – NOW. I thank thee for walking a piece with me."

I was specific and omitted references to any problems in the relationship which needed to be resolved. I placed everything in the positive, present-tense and didn't give voice to words like *can't, don't, won't, wouldn't, couldn't, shouldn't* and *not.* The only thought I was having was the image of the satisfying, loving relationship I had created by the power of divine love coupled with clear intent. In a later chapter, I provide sample claims for a number of common desires, but as always: *Do what works for you.*

8. SEE THE DESIRED OUTCOME IN ADVANCE.

Take a moment to really see the results of your wanding. Employ lots of detail. In the example of an improved relationship, you would visualize smiles, and kisses. See travel, hand holding and love-making. See it. Envision the sights, sounds, tastes, smells and textures which accompany your

successful result. This is the process of putting it out to the universe. Whatever your spirit lays claim to is instantly created. The next step is to let it go and trust that it has happened.

8. LET IT GO.

In wanding, you invoke the power of spirit in your behalf. But the outcome doesn't rely on your guide and the divine alone. You must make it real to your spirit. You mustn't merely believe the outcomes *will* come to pass, you get to trust that they already have come to pass. The notion of *instantaneous outcome* runs counter to conventional human wisdom and is a difficult mindset for mortal beings to overcome. You are the product of a lifetime's worth of pre-conceptions about the way things work. You don't conquer all that negativity and scarcity-based programming in a day. *Unless you do.* For most apprentice practitioners, trust in the

process comes with time and practice. The subtitle to this book calls wanding "The very new, very ancient *art* and *science* of boldly claiming the life, the love and the prosperity the universe stands ready to provide you." Wanding is a *science* from the standpoint that there is no "magic" to it in the carnival sense. It is established, objective fact like gravity. Release a coin in mid-air and it will tumble to the earth. Put forth your desires to the universe and they will be fulfilled. But the *art* aspect comes into it in the sense of an individual's ability to create maximum value through the proper preparation, spiritual attitude, clear intent, and trust in the process, the self, the guide, the universe, and God.

Don't be discouraged at perceived failures early in your wanding experience. It becomes second nature in time. But that brings us to the next point worth making: Will you know if you've been successful or not?

7 IT DOESN'T HAVE TO LOOK A CERTAIN WAY

One of the significant barriers to effective wanding involves mis-perception on the part of the practitioner. It's important to acknowledge the changes taking place all around you that result from putting forth your claim to the universe. It's like the old story of a man working on a roof. Hammering down a shingle, a roofer hit his thumb, lost his concentration, and started to roll down the steep gable of a very, very high roof. Not a particularly spiritual man under normal circumstances, this man instantly found religion.

"Spare me, oh Lord," he cried, gaining speed. "Spare me and I'll devote my life to good works. I'll give to the poor.

I'll clothe the naked and feed the hun –" Just as he was heading over the edge, his overalls got caught on a large nail poking out at the edge of the roof. The nail stopped his fall and his life was spared. As he dangled in the air twenty feet off the ground, the roofer looked up to heaven and said; "Never mind, Lord. I got it handled on my own."

With, or without our realizing it, miracles happen around us all the time. One need only pay attention to the signs in order to recognize the truth in the statement, "coincidences are no coincidence." I suggest that it's just as important to know *how* the universe works as it is to understand why it works.

The universe uses the laws of physics – *most of the time.* That is to say, popular fiction over-promises when it depicts a wizard waving a wand to make an evil castle disappear. If you were to put forth your claim to the universe that the castle needed to be removed, any number of things might

occur. The castle could get struck by lightening during a freak storm. There might be a fire within, or a flood without. An earthquake. A tornado. A local hoard of Huns could attack and destroy it. The evil force within could die, or move on, or find religion. Or, perhaps, you might wake up one morning and realize the castle has disappeared for *you* – that it just doesn't matter to you anymore.

The miracle of coincidence.

My wife and I are both in our second marriages. Here's a true incident which occurred during her first. One day, she decided that she deserved to own a Mercedes Benz *within the week.* At the time, she and her husband, Tony, were struggling with the financial pressures of homeownership and a new baby. Tony was building a business and money was tight. Her job as a dental assistant fell far short of ever

providing for such an extravagance. There was no rational reason to assume that she could step into a new Mercedes within five years, let alone one week. But she put forth her claim and let it go – trusting in the universal law of supply to deliver the car in any manner the universe saw fit. Excited, she told her husband, co-workers, and several of her friends that she'd be getting her new car within a few days. She even called her mother in a neighboring state and told her to clear her schedule for the joyride which would be taking place the following weekend.

Understandably skeptical, Tony laughed as he related the story to his business partner, Greg. Greg didn't laugh. Instead, Greg suggested that *his* car, a silver-gray Mercedes Benz, might serve as an appropriate bonus for Tony based on the recent quarter's successful financial numbers. And that was that. It hadn't even taken a week. Within three

days, my wife had her car – the shiny, new Mercedes she ultimately drove into the ground. The key to her success in this instance is that she hadn't placed any restrictions or conditions on how the universe might fulfill her request. It didn't have to look a certain way. She simply made her claim, let it go, trusted, and got her result. Now, most people observing this scenario would have said it was all a lucky coincidence. My wife knows better. So do I.

What follows is the transcript of a news story which ran on television in 1998. A group of us had decided to combine our spirit energies toward assisting the Honduran people in the wake of the devastation caused by Hurricane Mitch. The agreement was as follows: We would create a relief effort based solely on the power of divine love and our own clear intention. We wouldn't make it easy on ourselves by simply opening our wallets. The relief had to come from the uni-

verse and didn't have to look a certain way. We gave the universe a week. As it turned out, it only needed five days – and even threw in media coverage as a bonus. Here is the transcript of the television news story which aired 11/28.98:

Aid to Honduras
(11/28/98)

Nineteen-thousand people are still missing in the aftermath of Hurricane Mitch. And 3-million are homeless. News Specialist Tracey Butler reports the relief from Utah continues to head to Central America.

It's easy to feel overwhelmed and to simply tune out especially in the aftermath of a storm as destructive as Hurricane Mitch. But today, I met a group of people who -- in the middle of Thanksgiving week -- gave their all, so Hondurans may have the help they desperately need.

Sixty-five thousand pounds of medical supplies, beds, clothing and computer equipment are sorted and loaded by an army of volunteers. Most of the emergency supplies have been sitting at the Ogden Defense Depot in undelivered freight containers.

And that effort took nearly 40 volunteers less than a week. Last week a group of friends got together and decided they wanted to do something to help Hondurans after Hurricane Mitch. Five days later, this is the result.

Five semi-loads filled with supplies.

Evan Twede, Volunteer: "Not only did this happen in less than a week's time, but none of us had to work very hard – and look what we've got! Five semi loads full of vital supplies for Honduras."

Paula Wesson, Volunteer: "We were amazed at the outpouring of love from people that came from St. George from clear up to Brigham City. So many people came out from different church organizations. I don't know how everyone heard about it, but it's amazing."

Dan Marlon, Volunteer: "It's going to the first lady of Honduras. She is the one spearheading their donations there and distributing it."

The last box is loaded. And an intensive five day effort comes to an end. A local trucker is volunteering his time and gas money to drive the first load. And a final farewell for the long journey ahead.

Most of the supplies sitting in the Ogden Depot were either left over from auctions, unclaimed goods, or previously donated. There are hundreds of boxes still sitting in the warehouse - they will be donated to the Sub For Santa program.

The universe's response to our claim came in the form of five semi-loads of vital supplies which dropped neatly into our laps. Some people said it was a coincidence. Those

who knew better called it a miracle.

Recently, I realized I would need an additional ten thousand dollars to pay some unanticipated expenses. I put forth my claim of exactly ten thousand dollars to the universe and and let it go. I had ended the wanding session with the usual "NOW," but I hadn't anticipated that "NOW" would occur so quickly. Within the hour, two competing political campaigns from a distant state called me within ten minutes of each other. I explained to the first caller that my standard retainer fee was ten thousand dollars. He agreed. Ten minutes later, the second campaign coordinator called and I had to deliver the bad news that I had been "recently" retained by his competition. Minutes later, the first campaign called back and said that ten thousand was too steep for them to handle at that time. We settled on half that amount. I didn't feel short-changed by the universe or God. Nor did I worry. I

had made a claim on ten thousand and I still very much expected to receive the full amount. An hour later, a third campaign from within my home state called and offered me five thousand dollars to act as a consultant. Within two hours of making my claim, the funds I had requested were being forwarded to me by overnight courier. I have several dramatic examples of this process at work. The very book you hold is an example of the power of clear intent and trust.

As you wand, open yourself to all the possibilities. When things begin to happen in your life, be aware of how they are occurring, and what the effects are. Keep a journal. I have included several pages at the end of this book for that purpose, but I recommend you invest in something nice. *A Fulfillment Journal.* In it, write down your wanding experiences in detail. Include any messages or impressions you

receive while in a wanding session, while meditating, or while sleeping. Our guides speak to us as we sleep. Write down your dreams. Chronicle any "coincidences" which occur during the course of the day. Jot down the magnificent and insignificant. If you find yourself thinking of an acquaintance you haven't interacted with in years, only to discover a message from that person on your answering machine, make note of it. Over time, you will notice a pattern emerging between the claims you put out to the universe, and what you received as a result.

The universe is win/win.

Nobody likes a sore winner. About the time you start thinking more of others than you do of yourself, you will notice a profound change in the intensity and power present in your wanding. Remember, the universe exists solely to sup-

ply us what we deserve, desire and require. In common religious parlance, the universe pours forth *blessings.* Be open to devoting yourself and your energies to those around you. Give freely of your spiritual resources in the pursuit of peace, freedom and abundance for your communities whether they be local, national, or global. The act of wanding in behalf of strangers is one of the most electrifying, satisfying contributions you will ever make to the family of spirits currently playing out their lives in mortality. Do this, and your bond with the divine will take on entirely new, transcendently rich dimensions. Your communication with your guides will become infinitely more clear and direct. The cause and effect results of your wanding will take on a dramatic new quality. You will see the workings of spirit all around you. Share your spiritual gifts. I assure you it's a path worth pursuing.

8

WANDING APPLICATIONS

Here are a few standard wanding applications. These claims are simple and general, but should provide an outline for effective practice on your part. Once you get a feel for the language, the tone, and the essential methodology, you will discover your own unique style – one which suits your personal attitudes and preferences. I offer the following for reference:

Zipping up.

This is a daily ritual to align your centers of energy. Whether you believe in the concept of chakras or not, I strongly suggest you *Zip up* every morning.

Zipping up is accomplished with a simple motion which begins near your knees and ends over your head. Extend your wand outward, cross your arms into an "X" where your right hand is positioned roughly over your left knee and visa-versa. While moving your body and hands up toward the ceiling, uncross your arms in a fluid motion until your hands are over your head. Here is the claim:

"Divine love is doing its perfect work.

My energy is clear, powerful, aligned, and charged with spirit — Now!"

Perform this process whenever your energy appears weak.

Wealth.

It's important to remember that you don't have to qualify for material increase in your life. The universe was set up to provide you with whatever it takes for you to accomplish your goals in mortality. If you desire money, claim it. This is a very simple, very straightforward process.

After preparing yourself properly, bring forth your wand and draw the shape that represents material wealth to you.

Make this symbol at least five times, while voicing the following claim: *"Divine love is doing its perfect work. I boldly claim, declare and decree that money flows abundantly to me from expected and unexpected sources — Now!"* Remember to express your gratitude.

If you have a specific dollar amount in mind, incorpo-

rate that figure into your claim. Now visualize it. See the money coming into your life. Hear the laughter, and the joy that will accompany it. Picture the positive improvements the funds will bring you. See it. Smell it. Hear it.

That's the easy part. Here's the challenging part. You must let go of the little voice in your head telling you that it's impossible. Visualize that voice of doubt and dissension as an ugly, black bug. Feel free to step on it. If you're the non-violent type, place the noisy pest into a small wooden box and send it flying at the speed of thought over the house tops and trees – right out of your space. Repeat this process as often as necessary.

Remember, you have placed your claim into the capable care of the universe. Trust that what you have requested has already been created for you. Let go and let God.

Health.

This can be challenging. When you or a loved one is seriously ill, your spirit may be depressed and dampened to the point that clear, positive affirmation seems an insurmountable obstacle. This is normal. Under these conditions, it's wise to will brilliant light into the darkness your soul is experiencing. Imagine yourself in a dark cave. It's clammy, cold and populated with slithery, dank creatures. Now envision a point of light six inches in front of your face. Watch the light increase in size. Hear the shimmering, tinkling sound of it. Feel its warmth on your face as it completely engulfs the space you're in – swallowing you up whole. See how the light drives away the creatures of darkness, leaving only dry, loving, comforting warmth and peace. The cave now dissolves into your actual surroundings. Suddenly your world looks different. Everything around you is buzzing –

charged with the intense light of spirit. Bring forth your wand and draw a symbol which represents good health to you over the effected area of your body. Do this at least five times while you vocalize your claim. If you are wanding remotely for someone else, draw the same symbol while envisioning yourself standing before the person afflicted. Here is the accompanying claim for restored health and relief of pain: *"Divine love is doing its perfect work. I boldly claim, declare and decree that I (name) enjoy(s) health, vitality, strength, comfort, warmth and love — Now!"*

Now envision the source of the ailment as a fuzzy blob of color. With the power of your mind, pull that color right out of the affected area. Seal it mentally in a box, an envelope, or use what I use: a Ziploc bag. Then send it speeding from you over the buildings, trees and mountains. Let it go.

Recovering lost objects. There are few things in life as frustrating as losing a wallet, purse or your keys. I employed this claim last winter while shoveling snow. I had moved my son's car out of the driveway, placing his keys in the pocket of my new parka. It was almost an hour before I realized that what I thought was a pocket was actually a vent. The keys were nowhere to be found. My anxiety mounted as I combed the deep piles of snow with a rake. As much as I hated the thought of his car and house keys being out in the open where anyone could find them, the thing that really bothered me was admitting my stupidity in losing them. Then I had a sudden burst of clarity. Wand in hand, I made my claim. It went like this:

"Divine love is doing its perfect work. I boldly claim,

declare and decree that I am guided by spirit to uncover the covered and see the unseen. I have my (<u>object</u>) Now!"

I sketched the crude outline of a key five times as I made my claim, then took a deep breath and closed my eyes – waiting for the location to appear in my mind. Instead of visualizing it, I was spun on my heal – pulled directly to a location three feet off the ground, at the base of the driveway – a spot I'd previously raked. On impulse, I plunged the wand about a foot into the snow and instantly found metal. I have since come to realize that wanding can direct the practitioner to lost items either by physical means like dowsing, or spiritual means – that is, presenting the item's location in the mind's eye. The key to this process, like all others discussed, is trust. Don't allow your imagination to overwhelm the process. And don't have expectations regarding how the information will be presented. It doesn't have to look a certain way.

Spirit Communication.

I have two very good friends who have crossed over. In fact, this book is dedicated to them. I miss their physical presence in my life, but I am still treated to their laughter, bad jokes and spiritual insights on a regular basis. We tend to think of death as a door – a portal we walk through at the end of this mortal experience – a door that slams behind us – never to be opened again. Well, I can tell you that it has been one of

the most meaningful insights I've ever received to realize that the door to the world of spirit swings both ways.

Spirits of those you love will enter your space if you call them forth. They travel at the speed of thought – yours or theirs – and love to be recognized by the clues they leave. If you desire actual, literal communication, there are several

avenues for accomplishing it. Wanding provides an effective method.

Here is the claim: Draw a door with your wand. Repeat this five times while verbalizing the following:

"Divine love is doing its perfect work. I boldly claim, declare and decree that this doorway opens to the realms of spirit. I am in contact with (————) who has crossed. I feel his/her presence. I hear his/her words. I see his/her impressions — Now!"

Now, inverting your wand, symbolically "knock" on the door you've drawn three times, while invoking the name of the departed spirit in this fashion:

(Name) — I welcome and embrace thee.

(Name) — I welcome and entreat thee.

(Name) — I welcome and invite thee.

Communication with mortal beings requires a great deal of energy on the part of spirit. The form a message takes is entirely up to the individual and their abilities. Therefore, be open to anything that comes and watch carefully for clues. It is often helpful to elevate your own vibration to meet theirs. You accomplish this through meditation and mental imagery. See the reunion in your mind. Imagine it. Hear the sound of the departed spirit's voice or laughter. Envision this person as you last saw him/her in life. Create as complete a mental picture as you can. Feel your body buzzing and becoming lighter and less dense. Hold this thought for several minutes, then let it go.

Spirit energies, like mortal men and women, possess different capabilities. They will appear to you in the manner which best suits them. Communication, therefore, can take many forms. Don't miss a message from spirit because you

expected it to conform to your preconceptions, or to occur within your time frame. Communication comes when it comes. It appears in the way it appears. I can assure you that, over time, your method for communicating with spirit energies will take on a more casual, familiar quality. But it's like any other relationship. You have to learn how best to communicate.

You may see the person in a dream. They may present themselves through visual clues, smells, or through the manipulation of physical objects which had significance to them in life. You may suddenly hear a song that meant something to the both of you, or see a sign, or their name on a passing truck. You may look over one moment and find them sitting on your couch. Spirit energies often make effective use of electronic devices. Be open. Be certain to acknowledge anything your friend or loved-one in spirit

serves up for you. Make careful notes in the *Fulfillment Journal* at the back of this book. By doing this, you will spot trends, and, over time, learn the most effective method for both of you.

Remember that, although they are no longer in mortality, these are *people* you're dealing with. They don't exist simply to gratify your desires or perform endless tricks for you on demand. Treat them with respect.

In the same way that you let a ringing telephone go to voicemail when you're pressed for time, there are times when energies have something more pressing to accomplish than turning your stereo on and off in the middle of the night. Bear in mind that there are labors being performed and activities taking place on the other side, too. If you fail to establish contact on the first try, then try again later. Persistence will pay off.

Dismissing undesirable energies.

And, what do you do should unwanted energies take up residence in your house? There is a method for removing undesirable spirits which is very effective. The important thing to realize is that, contrary to what you find depicted in movies and on television, the power to command is yours – not the other way around. Often, energies become stuck between earth and the spirit world. They are known to gravitate after death to the types of activities and desires which were important to them in life. The truth is, the spirit world is all around us at this very moment. We as mortals are generally not aware of it, because we're not supposed to be. However, on those occasions when our two worlds intersect, it can be very unsettling. Here is a claim for removing a ghost or other unwanted presence in your home. It's instructive to realize that many of these energies may be confused as to their cur-

rent status. They may not realize that they are dead, or how much time has elapsed since their passing. For this reason, you must make an informative, imperative claim on your property. The claim goes as follows: With your wand extended over your head, draw a large "X" then encircle it. Repeat this five times while expressing the following:

"Divine love is doing its perfect work. I boldly claim, declare and decree that this property upon which I stand is hallowed for my use. The year is (current year.) You have crossed from mortality into spirit and may make no further claim on this space. I command you to seek the light and depart from this place — Now!"

Now, visualize this spirit entering the light. Envision a group of guides accompanying and assisting the unwanted energy

in its journey. This is literally what is happening on the other side. The entity may still refuse the embrace of the light, but the guardians will place a barrier between that spirit and your property. Send out thoughts of love and light. If you have a wand of sage available, smudge the area. Imagine the smoke as shimmering light which drives away the darkness. Then let it go.

Divining true and false answers.

Your wand is a powerful detector of truth and lies. It can provide you with yes or no answers and even spell out words and provide numbers and dates.

True or false: Invert the wand. Touch the thumb and middle finger of your dominant hand. Place them over the

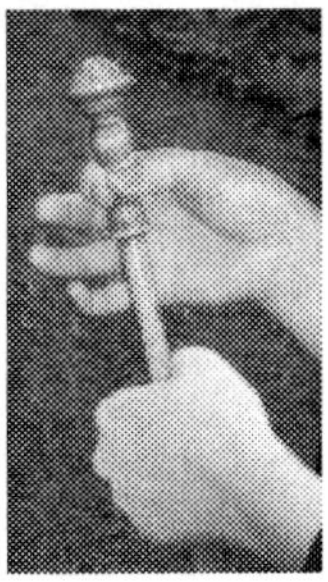

Fondel as shown. Grasp the Steck at the midpoint. Apply light pressure so the handle of your wand is pulling against the junction where your fingers meet. Make the following claim:

"Divine love is doing its perfect work. I discern the right from the wrong, the true from the false, the white from the black, the good from the evil, the yes from the no — Now!"

Pose your true or false question aloud. Now, with moderate force, push against your locked fingers with the handle

of the wand. If the junction breaks easily, the answer is false. If the junction holds firmly, the answer is true. This method works equally well for yes/no questions.

Words and numbers. To spell words, or determine numbers, a slightly different method is used. With the wand

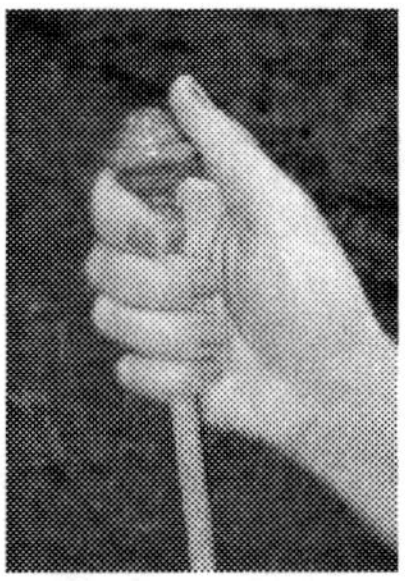

still inverted, grasp the handle with the fingers of your dominant hand – allowing the thumb to rest against the bulbous end of the Kell. The claim is the same as the aforementioned. The action is as follows: As you pose your question, begin to rub the rounded end of the Kell with your thumb – naming a letter or number with each stroke. When your thumb sticks noticeably, make note of that letter or number. Repeat this process until the effect ceases. The letters and numbers are received in sequence. Words are formed left to right. Numbers: 1's, 10's, 100's, etc.

Improving your memory.

You've noticed that your mind is a boundless repository of useless information until you really need it, haven't you? It happens to everybody. An arcane fact has been buzzing around in your head for weeks. Suddenly, at dinner, someone will ask; "Who was the original drummer for the Beatles?" You knew the answer ten seconds before you heard the question, but now you're drawing a blank. Here is a claim which will improve you memory instantly. Close your eyes and encircle your head five times while repeating the following:

"Divine love is doing its perfect work. All facts, figures, names, faces and places come to my mind the moment I require them. My memory is perfect — Now!"

And so it is. Envision your mind as the hull of a great ship. See the rivets and welds. Notice how no water gets in and

no air escapes to the ocean below. Your mind is as tight as that hull. Your memory functions as flawlessly as the well-oiled engine. You are a perfectly operating, closed system of pure knowledge. All facts are there when you need them. Out of mind when you don't. You'll be amazed at the difference this simple claim makes. By the way, before Ringo Starr, the four who were called fab consisted of John, Paul, George and Pete Best.

Invisibility.

I shouldn't admit this, but I wand myself protection from police radar. I envision a bubble of light over my car which is brilliant and intense to everyone but law enforcement personnel and their devices. To them, I am invisible. I do this in response to my natural tendency to appear guilty even when I'm not. Often, I would find myself creating elaborate scenarios in my mind in case I should ever be pulled over. And, all too frequently, discovered myself experiencing the very encounter – in precisely the manner I'd imagined it. I finally realized that I was not only visualizing trouble on the interstate in a very real, three-dimensional way – I was actively calling it forth. Today, while I continue to make an honest effort to obey all laws, I don't fret about blasting through speed traps. I visu-

alize protection from detection and I get it. It's better than a radar detector. This process can also be used in any circumstance where you feel at risk or don't wish to be noticed.

Here is the claim: Draw a circle of bright light around your car or your body. See it and hear it shimmer. Repeat the circle five times as you express the following:

"Divine love is doing its perfect work. I boldly claim, declare and decree that I am seen by those I would have see me. I am invisible to those who deserve no knowledge of me — Now!"

Now, see yourself slipping past the undesirable person or persons unnoticed. Visualize your smile of satisfaction. Feel your power. See it working for you. This claim is very effective in reducing the aura that fear and anxiety can create around you. People with ill intent are often very adept at picking up on this powerfully negative vibration. By wanding

yourself protection, you surround yourself with a cloak of confidence and superiority that dispels the outward appearance of fear.

Finding your soul mate.

This is different than the relationship claim mentioned earlier. It's a time-honored affirmation which is powerful in calling forth your soul mate. Here is the claim: Speak the following aloud while drawing the symbol five times which represents the gender of the person whom you seek.

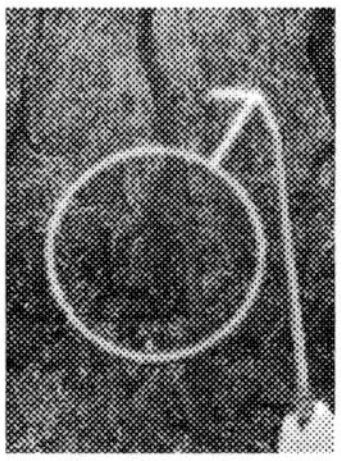

"Divine love is doing its perfect work. I boldly claim, declare, and decree that that which was promised in spirit, bound in spirit, and blessed in spirit, is now realized in flesh. My soul mate comes forth into my space to fulfill and complete me, to love and abide with me — Now!"

See this person in your mind. Imagine your guides reaching out and inspiring this person to find you. Feel the joys of your reunion. Offer this claim to the universe then let it go.

Creating a better relationship.

We covered this claim already as an example in an earlier chapter, but it deserves to be included in this list of wanding applications. What follows is the claim my wife created before we were married. She called forth every element of this claim, visualized it, and then let it go for the universe to deliver. I can tell you that our relationship embodies every detail of what she called forth. I recommend it to any couple interested in building a deep, lasting bond. It's never too early or too late to find bliss with your partner. Here is the claim. Draw a shape five times which symbolizes your desires. Tailor your claim to describe the relationship you're in search of. Here is an example:

"Divine love is doing its perfect work in my relationship with (name.) I boldly claim, declare, and decree that we experience an abundance of joy, excitement, unity, honesty,

adventure, friendship, passion, trust and love — Now!" Envision your successful union. Hear it. Smell it. Taste it. Make it real for you. Experience the joys of it – the hand holding, love making and laughter. See travel. See unity and love. State your claim to the universe then let it go.

Enhancing spiritual practices.

There are many aspects of the spiritual journey which can

be enhanced through the application of wanding: remote viewing, astral travel, scrying, lucid dreaming and card reading to name a few. Here is the claim: Speak the following aloud while drawing the symbol five times which represents the awakening of your spiritual senses, or opening of your third eye.

"Divine love is doing its perfect work. I boldly claim, declare, and decree that I see that which can only be seen without the physical eye. My spiritual senses are awake and charged with the power and light of spirit — Now!"

Imagine an eye in the center of your forehead parting its lids and blinking open. See the world of spirit vividly through this new sense. Offer this claim to the universe then let it go.

Weight Loss.

You create your reality moment to moment, but you can also

change your reality moment to moment. If conventional methods have failed you, wanding is an excellent way to bring about physical improvements.

While standing before a full-length mirror, sketch the outline of your desired shape at least five times. Here is the claim:

"Divine love is doing its perfect work. I boldly claim, declare, and decree that I appear in the flesh the way I create myself in the glass of this mirror and the glass of my mind— Now!"

Imagine the experiences you will have having shed the weight. See the approving glances from family, friends and co-workers. Hear the compliments. Experience your new-found

vitality. See yourself wearing the clothes you desire to wear. Envision the trip to Good Will Industries with all of the clothing which will never fit again. Now, normally, a claim ends by offering it to the universe and letting it go. Not so with in this circumstance. To further enhance the effectiveness of your claim, you must take symbolic action. Go out and buy an expensive outfit in your target size. Hang it in plain sight so that you encounter it at least twice a day. Each time you pass it, repeat this affirmation silently or vocally:

"Divine love is doing its perfect work. I boldly claim, declare, and decree that this is the clothing of my new body. I have my new body— Now! This outfit fits me perfectly — Now!"

Wanding for global peace.

In the past several pages, I've provided a format for creating

claims which covered the spectrum from lost objects and lost fat, to finding lost loves. I would be remiss, however, if I didn't put at least one claim into print aimed at improving the world. As I said previously, these claims are but a guide – make the words and symbols your own. Here is the claim: Draw an image which represents world peace, understanding and enlightenment to you. Repeat this symbol five times while repeating aloud:

"Divine love is doing its perfect work. I boldly claim, declare, and decree that love, understanding, light, and peace fall like rain into every corner of creation, upon every land, every tongue and every people — Now!"

See this dream becoming reality. Envision it, then let it go.

9 WANDING AND YOUR RELIGIOUS FAITH

It's the question I'm always asked: Can I wand and still remain a good Christian, Muslim, Buddhist or Jew? Does it place my soul in jeopardy to seek a personal relationship with a spirit guide, guardian angel, or the almighty? Here's my standard reply: The source of power in wanding is the same source in praying. It's all God. Yet, even in a technically advanced society which has brought us the mapping of the human genome, the micro processor and the DVD, the old superstitions and misunderstandings endure. In 1692, twenty innocent people were put to death as witches in New England. The inquisition killed and tortured thousands. In

the early 1840's the Mormon prophet Joseph Smith was shot and killed for claiming to have spoken with God. Jesus Christ was nailed to a cross on Golgotha for upsetting the Jewish apple cart. Gandhi. Joan of Arc. Perpetua. Thomas More. Imam Hussain. Our planet's history is written in the blood of the decent, honest seekers of truth because of an attitude which has endured for eons: "Whosoever is not of me is of the devil."

The devil in the details.

Today, the modern religion of witchcraft, Wicca, has devoted considerable resources to dispelling the institutionally thorny belief that their practice of earth magic is merely a front for worship of the beast. While cults do exist throughout the world which are dedicated to the worship of demonic spirits, they have no more relationship to Wicca than they

do to classical Christianity or Buddhism. But the "devil" still manages to get his licks in. All the world's great religions claim, subtly or overtly, to possess an exclusive pathway to God. Therefore, it follows that if you're not in the *true* church, you must be in a *false* church. The devil's church.

Every path leads to God.

That's not to imply religion is undesirable. For earnest seekers, religion provides the ritual, doctrine and sense of the divine which allows them to throw off the heavy vibrations of mortality and commune at a more comfortable, familiar frequency. The spirit energy created in mass worship, reminds the soul of its real home. To some, religion possesses all the answers to life's great questions and is the culmination of the spiritual journey. For others, formal worship is a starting point, a foundation which provides a basis

for deeper, independent study of the mysteries of God and the universe. Though many religions have made the uneasy transition into the modern world, the core doctrines remain etched in the slow stone of tradition and are mired in centuries-old attitudes and prejudices. And that's where religion runs into itself. Birth control, divorce, the reading of certain scientific texts, allowing females an equal voice in political and religious affairs. All sins.

Whether you should or should not wand, play with face cards, or shave your facial hair, is a personal choice. But be mindful. If you've ever been to a psychic, purchased a lotto ticket, prayed standing up, or sought the assistance of a homeopathic physician, your soul may already be imperiled. If you've allowed your daughter to talk back to you and haven't beaten her with a rod, if you've logged onto the internet, or exposed your ankle in public, you are a candi-

date for Hell's fiery wind. If you've cut your hair, permitted a confessed homosexual to live, had a cup of coffee, or purchased an electronic device, you could be beyond the reach of salvation. The point is clear. If you're breathing, you're sinning by one religious standard or another at this very moment. The question of right and wrong is just too broad, and the opinions and viewpoints too culturally and ideologically charged. In the eternal realms, things are simpler. There is no right and wrong. There is what works and what doesn't. So, what works for you? Your path is solely your own. How you express yourself, seek truth, or commune with spirit is a personal, sacred matter. Wanding is directed, affirmative spiritual energy which draws upon the power of divine love – like prayer. God is only about love and acceptance – though you would never come to that conclusion based on what you hear while warming a pew.

So much of what religious dogma tells us about God can't be true. Any being with the inspired, aesthetic impulse to create something as complex, symmetrical and beautiful as the common ragweed couldn't possibly hate a creature as magnificent as man. The following example illustrates the God taught in many churches, mosques and synagogues.

I have five children. Their ages range from eighteen to ten. I love them so much that I allow them to stumble from time to time, dry their tears when they need it, and do my best to provide for their well-being. If I had taken the traditional God approach to my parenting, I would have whisked my youngsters off to Italy years ago and hidden their return tickets and passports somewhere in Europe. With loving tears I would have explained to my precious ones that despite their inability to speak the language, and despite the fact that I had left no clues whatsoever as to the where-

abouts of the important documents, I nevertheless expected them, as inexperienced children, to read my mind, find the tickets and passports and return home. With a kindly wink, I'd have pointed out that should they fail in their task, their names would be blotted from my will and their existence in the family forgotten. As a parting shot I would have assured them that I'd be watching their every move and that even if they should, by some stroke of luck, make it back to me, they'd be made to suffer for every mis-step along the way.

The analogy is ludicrous. So is the belief that a being of God's attainment would be mired in such negative, blatantly human predispositions. If you take nothing more out of this book than the knowledge that you are acceptable to God exactly as you are, and that there is nothing more for you to do, then reading it will have been worthwhile. The judgment after this life is not a trial where you must defend your salva-

tion amid the taunts of those who managed a more obedient existence. It's a review – a period of personal reflection wherein you determine whether you met your objectives in coming to earth and what the end result was. Souls are never in jeopardy. The purpose of life is to experience ourselves and to grow in love. To that end, and that end only, the universe was created.

The spirit does not fear God because it knows God.

10

HEALING THE WORLD

The world looks vastly different today than it did when I was born four decades ago. To those claiming that we, as a society, are no more civilized or evolved than the cave-men, I offer a qualified rebuttal. The world *is* different. Our consciousness is rising. Seeds of spirituality, which have been tossed on the wind for decades, are now taking root throughout our global community. The result is a beautiful, tenacious little weed called enlightenment.

The sixties brought about significant shift and upheaval in traditional values. For the first time, vast populations experimented with their newfound freedom to question. Authority. Religion. Societal values. Conventional wisdom.

The *revolution of self* was just the latest milestone in a long line of evolutionary baby-steps which have been shepherding us toward our ultimate destiny as a society – a golden age of spiritual understanding and enlightenment. Where THE QUESTION exists, evolution follows.

I'm just barely old enough to remember the early civil rights demonstrations in America. I was raised in a family where God, country, and the superiority of the white race were a given – like breathing. My parents weren't racists, or Nazis. They were merely a product of the prevailing attitudes of their day: God-fearing, Bible-toting Americans – suburbs away from ever experiencing an impulse to ask THE QUESTION: "How do we support, condone or justify the ill treatment of men, woman and children based solely on the color of their skin?" Old prejudices die hard. But die they do. The men, women and institutions which have faith-

fully nourished negative racial attitudes in the past are now, themselves, teetering between the rest-home and the grave. Today's emerging indigo generation has a more enlightened, inclusive take on things.

We were discussing music one night at dinner when my teenage daughter, a beautiful blond with ambitions to sing, complained that because she hadn't been born black, she felt short-changed. She said that everybody who was anybody these days was black – and that it wasn't fair to have been born white. I've heard this comment a lot in her circle.

People of color the world over still suffer unacceptable levels of prejudice, ignorance and hatred based on the shade of their skin. But attitudes are changing. They're changing because people began to ask THE QUESTION. The old answers no longer make sense. They don't hold up under the harsh light of tough, new questions.

Within a generation or two, issues of skin color, religious affiliation, political persuasion, sexual orientation and ethnic origin will be as irrelevant to the family of man as the differences between our official state birds are to us today. Prejudice won't make sense in a world where people recognize themselves for what they really are: Beings who are one with everything in the universe – including God.

People who possess the knowledge of who they are, where they came from, why they're here, and where they're going, view the world differently. They perceive the unity in all they see around them rather than the differences. Because they have tasted love and acceptance, they are free to love and be accepting. They are not judged, and so, are relieved of the burden of formulating judgments about others. Abundance has eliminated scarcity from their lives – and with it, the tendency toward materialism, greed, and com-

petition. Their lives are a universal win/win.

There are those among you today who comprehend and apply these concepts. They are powerful people leading powerful, fulfilling lives – lives which are making a difference for themselves, their families and their communities.

If I could wave a wand and plant these same seeds of universal love and abundance into the hearts of every man, woman and child, scarcity, greed, anger and hate would end abruptly. If everyone – from the captain of industry, to the parish priest, the child in the school yard, or the inmate within prison walls – could catch even a fleeting glimpse of their own extraordinary power and potential, petty squabbles over baubles and borders would seem meaningless. Jealousy, envy, and greed would go the way of the other deadly sins. Light would drive away the darkness – leaving in its wake a new age of global spirituality and progress.

Fortunately, I *can* wave a wand. As can you.

I brought the practice of wanding public because you deserve its power in your life. As you learn to create maximum value through the expression of it, the implications for the human family will be profound. Wanding can lead to a personal relationship with the creator which will influence every aspect and perception in your life. Your light will shine in a way that's impossible to conceal. In sharing your experiences among your circle, your ripple effect will be enormous – "like a match in dry brush." Or so I've been told by a diverse group of messengers, living and dead.

Persistence from the other side.

Years ago, I was at a Denny's in Bellevue, Washington, with my wife and two oldest children. After breakfast, I got up to pay the check.

"Excuse me," a large, nicely dressed man said in a soft baritone. "This is not something I normally do, and I hope you won't think I'm crazy, but I have to ask – are you a minister of some sort?" I smiled and told him no. I didn't know what his business was, but he didn't strike me as a kook. His wife, still seated in their booth, appeared a bit embarrassed, but supportive as he spoke.

"I've dreamed about you," he said. "You have a mission. God has a work for you. I saw you preaching to thousands of people. I guess I was supposed to find you and tell you that." His words loosed a cold, tingling rush which coursed through my body. After apologizing for the intrusion, the man returned to his seat – flustered. My family was flustered as well – following me out of the restaurant with their mouths agape. It reminded me of an experience long forgotten, and at the time, misunderstood. While serving my

church during the period between high school and college, I encountered a man walking along the boardwalk in Emmerich, Germany. He passed me, then turned and followed me at a distance. When he finally spoke, he asked me if I believed in magic. I responded by *magically* pulling a German dime from his ear. "You have the magic," he said, earnestly but with a cheerful smile. "And it *will* find you."

Some months after the Denny's experience, a woman approached me in a crowded mall with a similar message. She stated, very matter-of-factly, that something big was about to catch up with me – that my efforts would help "heal the world."

I was in the same mall Christmas shopping one Saturday afternoon and noticed a psychic on duty at the new age bookstore. When I brushed past him he asked; "Are you wearing...sandlewood?" I sniffed the air. "Not me."

"It's just that, *sandlewood* is the scent I get when I'm in the presence of a master." I took the open seat. "You're going to write something," he said, "something important." adding that it would be successful – "but not just in the way many think of success."

Wanding has shaped my spiritual life and fulfilled my desires, but I hadn't planned to bring it public. I didn't feel it was my place to put it in print. One January night, that all changed.

During meditation, I had enjoyed a profoundly powerful and interesting spiritual experience. I remained in the dim light of my study pondering its implications when a breath of cold raised the hackles on my neck – a familiar indication that Gary, my deceased friend, had stopped in for a visit. Suddenly, a burst of inspiration flooded my mind – punctuated by a ringing in my ears which lasted for several

minutes. When my head cleared, I switched on my computer and began typing like I was taking dictation. I punched away into the evening, emerging the following morning with most of what is now called *WANDING*. Within a few days, I had completed the first draft. After reading it a few times, and passing it around to my circle for approval, I placed the manuscript on my desk – where it lay undisturbed for the next several months. I felt no urgency to actually publish it.

In April, I had an opportunity to visit with a well-known medium who had published a book chronicling her near-death experiences and the unique gifts she'd gained as a result. As a psychic, she was extraordinarily talented.

Her oxygen system clicked rhythmically as she spoke in quiet tones with a hint of a Tennessee drawl. "You didn't come alone," she said. "You've brought *somebody* with you." Then she said his name. "Gary's here." Within moments she

was receiving impressions about a small book which I would shortly put into print – the content of which had caught up to me through my own experiences over the course of many lifetimes. "This is something the world needs, Sugar," she said between halted breaths. "People need to hear your words." I told her about the book, but admitted that I still had some doubts about bringing it to a mass audience. The direct quote from Gary, who by that point in the reading had been joined by my other departed friend, Jeff, was; "Stop sweatin' the small stuff. Get off your butt and get moving with it."

The diminutive woman urged to me to trust my spirit and stop relying on my ego – that same ego telling me that no one would be interested in a how-to manual on wand-ing.

The final push came in June. We were browsing through

a spiritual bookstore downtown and felt ourselves drawn to George, the resident card/palm reader. He got right to the point.

"If you don't publish that book now," he stressed, my wife emphatically nodding in agreement, "the opportunity will pass." I finally understood. Wanding wouldn't wait.

The revelation in the wand.

I've been charged with bringing this powerful, spiritual practice to as many as I can. Wanding is but one tool for our growth as an emerging, spiritual society. There are, and will continue to be, several others – all provided to shepherd mankind into the next phase of our evolution. It occurred to me that the five elements represented in the wand both parallel and predict the human experience on earth.

As a species of primitive hunter-gatherers, we crawled,

walked, ran and rode through our EARTH phase – spreading nomadically across the habitable skin of the virgin planet. The revelation of WATER brought us cultivation, irrigation, reliable food supplies, language, philosophy, global commerce, and stable societies. Progress, wrought in the belching furnaces of industry, transported man into FIRE on wheels of steel. Today, we dwell in AIR. Our technology, clean, light and efficient, has provided the means to gather the tatters of our fragmented human family into a single, beautiful tapestry – a global community. We live in an age of marvels where breakthroughs in medicine, science, ideals and ideas leap instantly across continents – borne on the silent, sudden wings of satellites. All of it serves a purpose.

And now we stand on the verge of mankind's next and greatest evolutionary leap: SPIRIT – a day when the application and understanding of spiritual gifts, inspiration,

and psychic phenomena will be as ubiquitous, mundane, and ordinary as radio waves, telephones and microwave ovens seem to us now.

The age of SPIRIT dawned with a single whisper. Very few had ear enough to hear it. Today, voices from around the world are combining to create a chorus of enlightenment, empowerment, truth and love which will one day conquer the most distant and daunting frontier of them all: The human heart. Each of us has our own part to play in this spiritual awakening – and our own voice to add.

Heal yourself then heal others.

I'm assured through spirit that the information presented here is sufficient to bring you to an awareness of your own importance, prestige and position in the universe. And your power. The truth is, you are powerful beyond measure – an

essential truth you've been programmed to ignore. Wanding is a method for overcoming the ego's resistance to what the spirit knows is possible. It's spiritual connection for the spiritually challenged – a key to the law of universal supply granted to us without limitation by the source of divine love without end.

Wanding has changed my life in all the important ways. I'm grateful to those who brought it to me at the perfect time and in the perfect way. It has made my journey authentic and meaningful. It has filled my heart with love and acceptance. It has shown me the true nature of mortality and of the creator – a being who wouldn't have us any other way.

The power is, and has always been, yours. I urge you to use that power in behalf of those around you. Share your knowledge. When your spirit is healed, work to heal others.

I offer my best wishes to you in what I'm confident will be

an amazing spiritual adventure. May your path be blessed.

I thank you for walking a piece with me.

– Evan Twede

Be part of this spiritual awakening.
"Wood Works" is currently underway.
If you'd like your inspirational wanding experiences to be included, forward them to: author@lostwoodarts.com

For information about The Fitchel Society, wands, or to acquire an authentic Fitchel & Sons product, visit their site at: www.fitchel.com

FULFILLMENT JOURNAL

Fulfillment Journal

DAY ONE

Experiences of Spirit

DREAMS

Messages from Spirit

Fulfillment Journal

DAY TWO

Experiences of Spirit

DREAMS

Messages from Spirit

Fulfillment Journal

DAY THREE

Experiences of Spirit

DREAMS

Messages from Spirit

Fulfillment Journal

DAY FOUR

Experiences of Spirit

DREAMS

Messages from Spirit

Fulfillment Journal

DAY FIVE

Experiences of Spirit

DREAMS

Messages from Spirit

Fulfillment Journal

DAY SIX

Experiences of Spirit

DREAMS

Messages from Spirit

Fulfillment Journal

DAY SEVEN

Experiences of Spirit

DREAMS

Messages from Spirit

Fulfillment Journal

DAY EIGHT

Experiences of Spirit

DREAMS

Messages from Spirit

Fulfillment Journal

DAY NINE

Experiences of Spirit

DREAMS

Messages from Spirit

Fulfillment Journal

DAY TEN

Experiences of Spirit

DREAMS

Messages from Spirit

Fulfillment Journal

DAY ELEVEN

Experiences of Spirit

DREAMS

Messages from Spirit

Fulfillment Journal

DAY TWELVE

Experiences of Spirit

DREAMS

Messages from Spirit

Fulfillment Journal

DAY THIRTEEN

Experiences of Spirit

DREAMS

Messages from Spirit

Fulfillment Journal

DAY FOURTEEN

Experiences of Spirit

DREAMS

Messages from Spirit

Fulfillment Journal

DAY FIFTEEN

Experiences of Spirit

DREAMS

Messages from Spirit

Fulfillment Journal

DAY SIXTEEN

Experiences of Spirit

DREAMS

Messages from Spirit

Fulfillment Journal

DAY SEVENTEEN

Experiences of Spirit

DREAMS

Messages from Spirit

Fulfillment Journal

DAY EIGHTEEN

Experiences of Spirit

DREAMS

Messages from Spirit

Fulfillment Journal

DAY NINETEEN

Experiences of Spirit

DREAMS

Messages from Spirit

Fulfillment Journal

DAY TWENTY

Experiences of Spirit

DREAMS

Messages from Spirit

Fulfillment Journal

DAY TWENTY ONE

Experiences of Spirit

DREAMS

Messages from Spirit

Fulfillment Journal

DAY TWENTY TWO

Experiences of Spirit

DREAMS

Messages from Spirit

Fulfillment Journal

DAY TWENTY THREE

Experiences of Spirit

DREAMS

Messages from Spirit

Fulfillment Journal

DAY TWENTY FOUR

Experiences of Spirit

DREAMS

Messages from Spirit

Fulfillment Journal

DAY TWENTY FIVE

Experiences of Spirit

DREAMS

Messages from Spirit

Fulfillment Journal

DAY TWENTY SIX

Experiences of Spirit

DREAMS

Messages from Spirit

Fulfillment Journal

DAY TWENTY SEVEN

Experiences of Spirit

DREAMS

Messages from Spirit

Fulfillment Journal

DAY TWENTY EIGHT

Experiences of Spirit

DREAMS

Messages from Spirit

Fulfillment Journal

DAY TWENTY NINE

Experiences of Spirit

DREAMS

Messages from Spirit

Fulfillment Journal

DAY THIRTY

Experiences of Spirit

DREAMS

Messages from Spirit